1, 2 CORINTHIANS

BOOKS OF FAITH SERIES
Leader Session Guide

Ritva H. Williams

Minneapolis

1, 2 CORINTHIANS
Leader Session Guide

Books of Faith Series
Book of Faith Adult Bible Studies

Copyright © 2011 Augsburg Fortress. All rights reserved. Except for brief quotations in critical articles or reviews, no part of this book may be reproduced in any manner without prior written permission from the publisher. For more information, visit: www.augsburgfortress.org/copyrights or write to: Permissions, Augsburg Fortress, Box 1209, Minneapolis, MN 55440-1209.

 Book of Faith is an initiative of the
Evangelical Lutheran Church in America
God's work. Our hands.

For more information about the Book of Faith initiative, go to www.bookoffaith.org.

Scripture quotations, unless otherwise marked, are from New Revised Standard Version Bible, copyright © 1989 Division of Christian Education of the National Council of Churches of Christ in the United States of America. Used by permission. All rights reserved.

References to ELW are from *Evangelical Lutheran Worship* (Augsburg Fortress, 2006).

Web site addresses are provided in this resource for your use. These listings do not represent an endorsement of the sites by Augsburg Fortress, nor do we vouch for their content for the life of this resource.

ISBN: 978-1-4514-0144-8

Writer: Ritva H. Williams
Cover and interior design: Spunk Design Machine, spkdm.com
Typesetting: Timothy W. Larson, Minneapolis, MN

The paper used in this publication meets the minimum requirements of American National Standard for Information Sciences—Permanence of Paper for Printed Library Materials, ANSI Z329.48-1984.

Manufactured in the U.S.A.
14 13 12 11   1 2 3 4 5 6 7 8 9 10

CONTENTS

Introduction	5
1 Whose Am I? *1 Corinthians 1:1-30*	9
2 What Then Am I? *1 Corinthians 3:1—4:5*	18
3 It's Not All about Me? *1 Corinthians 6:12-20; 10:23-33*	27
4 What Am I Good For? *1 Corinthians 12:1-31*	36
5 What Will I Be Ultimately? *1 Corinthians 15:12-28, 35-58*	45
6 How Do I Achieve This Glory? *2 Corinthians 3:1—4:15*	55
7 What Can I Do Here and Now? *2 Corinthians 4:16—5:21*	65
8 What Is My Response to God's Grace? *2 Corinthians 8:1-15; 9:1-15*	73

Introduction

Book of Faith Adult Bible Studies

Welcome to the conversation! The Bible study resources you are using are created to support the bold vision of the Book of Faith initiative that calls "the whole church to become more fluent in the first language of faith, the language of Scripture, in order that we might live into our calling as a people renewed, enlivened, empowered, and sent by the Word."

Simply put, this initiative and these resources invite you to "Open Scripture. Join the Conversation."

We enter into this conversation based on the promise that exploring the Bible deeply with others opens us to God working in and through us. God's Word is life changing, church changing, and world changing. Lutheran approaches to Scripture provide a fruitful foundation for connecting Bible, life, and faith.

A Session Overview

Each session is divided into the following four key sections. The amount of time spent in each section may vary based on choices you make. The core Learner Session Guide is designed for 50 minutes. A session can be expanded to as much as 90 minutes by using the Bonus Activities that appear in the Leader Session Guide.

- **Gather (10-15 minutes)**

Time to check in, make introductions, review homework assignments, share an opening prayer, and use the Focus Activity to introduce learners to the Session Focus.

- **Open Scripture (10-15 minutes)**

The session Scripture text is read using a variety of methods and activities. Learners are asked to respond to a few general questions. As leader, you may want to capture initial thoughts or questions on paper for later review.

- **Join the Conversation (25-55 minutes)**

Learners explore the session Scripture text through core questions and activities that cover each of the four perspectives (see diagram on p. 6). The core Learner Session Guide material may be expanded through use of the Bonus Activities provided in the Leader Session Guide. Each session ends with a brief Wrap-up and prayer.

- **Extending the Conversation (5 minutes)**

Lists homework assignments, including next week's session Scripture text. The leader may choose one or more items to assign for all. Each session also includes additional Enrichment options and may include For Further Reading suggestions.

A Method to Guide the Conversation

Book of Faith Adult Bible Studies has three primary goals:

- To increase biblical fluency;
- To encourage and facilitate informed small group conversation based on God's Word; and
- To renew and empower us to carry out God's mission for the sake of the world.

To accomplish these goals, each session will explore one or more primary Bible texts from four different angles and contexts—historical, literary, Lutheran, and devotional. These particular ways of exploring a text are not new, but used in combination they provide a full understanding of and experience with the text.

Complementing this approach is a commitment to engaging participants in active, learner-orientated Bible conversations. The resources call for prepared leaders to facilitate learner discovery, discussion, and activity. Active learning and frequent engagement with Scripture will lead to greater biblical fluency and encourage active faith.

1 We begin by reading the Bible text and reflecting on its meaning. We ask questions and identify items that are unclear. We bring our unique background and experience to the Bible, and the Bible meets us where we are.

5 We return to where we started, but now we have explored and experienced the Bible text from four different dimensions. We are ready to move into the "for" dimension. We have opened Scripture and joined in conversation for a purpose. We consider the meaning of the text for faithful living. We wonder what God is calling us (individually and as communities of faith) to do. We consider how God's Word is calling us to do God's work in the world.

Devotional Context

Historical Context

Lutheran Context

Literary Context

2* We seek to understand the world of the Bible and locate the setting of the text. We explore who may have written the text and why. We seek to understand the particular social and cultural contexts that influenced the content and the message. We wonder who the original audience may have been. We think about how these things "translate" to our world today.

4 We consider the Lutheran principles that help ground our interpretation of the Bible text. We ask questions that bring those principles and unique Lutheran theological insights into conversation with the text. We discover how our Lutheran insights can ground and focus our understanding and shape our faithful response to the text.

3* We pay close attention to how the text is written. We notice what kind of literature it is and how this type of literature may function or may be used. We look at the characters, the story line, and the themes. We compare and contrast these with our own understanding and experience of life. In this interchange, we discover meaning.

* Sessions may begin with either Historical Context or Literary Context.

The diagram on p. 6 summarizes the general way this method is intended to work. A more detailed introduction to the method used in Book of Faith Adult Bible Studies is available in *Opening the Book of Faith* (Augsburg Fortress, 2008).

The Learner Session Guide

The Learner Session Guide content is built on the four sections (see p. 5). The content included in the main "Join the Conversation" section is considered to be the core material needed to explore the session Scripture text. Each session includes a Focus Image that is used as part of an activity or question somewhere within the core session. Other visuals (maps, charts, photographs, and illustrations) may be included to help enhance the learner's experience with the text and its key concepts.

The Leader Session Guide

For easy reference, the Leader Session Guide contains all the content included in the Learner Session Guide and more. The elements that are unique to the Leader Session Guide are the following:

- **Before You Begin**—Helpful tips to use as you prepare to lead the session.
- **Session Overview**—Contains detailed description of key themes and content covered in each of the four contexts (Historical, Literary, Lutheran, Devotional). Core questions and activities in the Learner Session Guide are intended to emerge directly from this Session Overview.
- **Key Definitions**—Key terms or concepts that appear in the Session Overview may be illustrated or defined.
- **Facilitator's Prayer**—To help the leader center on the session theme and leadership task.
- **Bonus Activities**—Optional activities included in each of the four sections of "Join the Conversation" used by the leader to expand the core session.
- **Tips**—A variety of helpful hints, instructions, or background content to aid leadership facilitation.
- **Looking Ahead**—Reminders to the leader about preparation for the upcoming session.

Leader and Learner

In Book of Faith Adult Bible Studies, the leader's primary task is facilitating small group conversation and activity. These conversations are built around structured learning tasks. What is a structured learning task? It is an open question or activity that engages learners with new content and the resources they need to respond. Underlying this structured dialog approach are three primary assumptions about adult learners:

- Adult learners bring with them varied experiences and the capability to do active learning tasks;
- Adult learners learn best when they are invited to be actively involved in learning; and
- Adults are more accountable and engaged when active learning tasks are used.

Simply put, the goal is fluency in the first language of faith, the language of Scripture. How does one become fluent in a new language, proficient in building houses, or skilled at hitting a baseball? By practicing and doing in a hands-on way. Book of Faith Adult Bible Studies provide the kind of hands-on Bible exploration that will produce Bible-fluent learners equipped to do God's work in the world.

Books of Faith Series

Book of Faith Adult Bible Studies include several series and courses. This 1, 2 Corinthians unit is part of the Books of Faith Series, which is designed to explore key themes and texts in the books of the Bible. Each book of the Bible reveals a unique story or message of faith. Many core themes and story lines and characters are shared by several books, but each book in its own right is a book of faith. Exploring these books of faith in depth opens us to the variety and richness of God's written word for us.

1, 2 Corinthians Unit Overview

In 1 and 2 Corinthians we find correspondence from the apostle Paul to the early church in Corinth. Paul's letters to this church provided guidance—for persons new to the faith as well as those growing in faith—about what it means to be a disciple of Jesus Christ. These letters continue to provide guidance to us today, as we face many of the same "big questions" as the early Christians.

Session One (1 Corinthians 1:1-30) asks, "Whose Am I?" In baptism we are claimed by Christ for God.

Session Two (1 Corinthians 3:1—4:5) asks, "What Then Am I?" We are all servants, laborers working together in God's field and on God's building, the temple. Each one of us is also part of God's field and temple that needs planting, watering, and building up.

Session Three (1 Corinthians 6:12-20; 10:23-33) asks, "It's Not All about Me?" Freedom in Christ is not permission for selfish indulgence. Freedom in Christ liberates us for service to the other.

Session Four (1 Corinthians 12:1-31) asks, "What Am I Good For?" The Holy Spirit gives each person a gift that is indispensable to the body of Christ.

Session Five (1 Corinthians 15:12-28, 35-58) asks, "What Will I Be Ultimately?" In the resurrection we will be like Christ and with Christ in God who will be all in all.

Session Six (2 Corinthians 3:1—4:15) asks, "How Do I Achieve This Glory?" Our transformation into the image of Christ is entirely the work of the Holy Spirit.

Session Seven (2 Corinthians 4:16—5:21) asks, "What Can I Do Here and Now?" In Christ we are invited to participate in God's mission of reconciliation.

Session Eight (2 Corinthians 8:1-15; 9:1-15) asks, "What Is My Response to God's Grace?" God's grace produces blessings. Our response is gratitude in the form of thanksgiving to God and generosity toward those in need.

SESSION ONE

1 Corinthians 1:1-30

Leader Session Guide

Focus Statement

In baptism we are claimed by Christ for God.

Key Verse

[God] is the source of your life in Christ Jesus, who became for us wisdom from God, and righteousness and sanctification and redemption. 1 Corinthians 1:30

Focus Image

© Brendan Hunter / iStockphoto

Whose Am I?

Session Preparation

Before You Begin . . .

Take a moment to reflect on the key question of the session: "Whose Am I?" Who or what claims you, your time, and your energies every day? Do they wear you down? Remember you are baptized! The good news is that in baptism Christ has claimed you for God, who is the source of your vitality. Let God be the center of your life, and all those other claims will settle into their proper places.

Session Instructions

1. Read this Session Guide completely and highlight or underline any portions you wish to emphasize with the group. Note any Bonus Activities you wish to do.

2. If you plan to do any special activities, check to see what materials you'll need, if any.

3. Have extra Bibles on hand in case a member of the group forgets to bring one.

Session Overview

Paul's Corinthian correspondence provides guidance for persons new to the faith, as well as those growing in faith, about what it means to be a disciple of Jesus Christ. Your group will discover that contemporary believers face many of the same "big questions" as the first Christians, even though the specific issues have changed. We begin this session where Paul began, exploring the questions, "Whose are you? To whom do you belong?"

LITERARY CONTEXT

Your group will begin by considering what kind of text you are studying. First Corinthians is a letter from Paul to the congregation in Corinth. This means that it is part of an ongoing long-distance relationship between Paul and members of this church. Reading it is like listening in on one side of a telephone conversation.

In the opening chapters Paul responds to an oral report received from "Chloe's people" (1:11) about the formation of competitive cliques. It appears that some members are boasting about

SESSION ONE

> **? Wisdom:**
> A well-thought-out understanding of the meaning and purpose of life, with a plan of action for how to succeed in life. The most popular wisdom (philosophy) in Paul's day was Stoicism, which asserted that one could achieve peace of mind by accepting that everything happens for a reason and everything is just as it should be. Greek and Roman elites were particularly drawn to this form of wisdom because it preserved their positions in the social order. In such a social system, ordinary people could achieve success only by attaching themselves to the powerful and wealthy. Paul contrasts this worldly wisdom with the wisdom of God as demonstrated in the cross of Christ.

"belonging to" the person who baptized them, for example, Paul, Apollos, or Cephas, while others seem content to boast that they belong to Christ (1:10-16).

Paul has two responses to this situation. First, he describes the members of the church in his initial greeting and thanksgiving. For example, he says that they are the "church of God," "sanctified in Christ Jesus," "saints" (1:2). The "grace of God" has been given them "in Christ Jesus," and they are "enriched in him" so that they lack no spiritual gift (1:7). Yet not many of them are wise, powerful, or of noble birth by human standards (1:26). Second, Paul contrasts worldly **wisdom**, that is, cultural understandings of how to live successfully, with the message about the cross of Christ.

Group members will be asked to reflect on what Paul is saying about who they really belong to, and what that might mean in their lives.

Historical Context

Participants will take a second look at this text through the historical lens of Greco-Roman cultural values. We can better understand the motives of the Corinthian church members by recognizing that they were raised in a society that viewed honor—the public recognition of status and prestige—as a primary value. Nobly born men, who were inevitably the best educated and politically powerful members of society, lorded over men of lower status, women, children, and slaves. These lower-status persons found a measure of prestige and pride by being publicly attached to such men as their kin, friends, employees, and dependents of various sorts.

Some Corinthian Christians were ranking the persons who had baptized them according to these cultural values. Apollos's cosmopolitan background and eloquence appealed to some (Acts 18:24—19:1), while others wanted to lift up Cephas (whose Greek name was Peter), the leader of the apostles and pillar of the Jerusalem church (Galatians 1:18—2:14). Paul refuses to play their game, insisting that God is not interested in Greco-Roman social prestige and honor.

As the group examines the behavior of the first-century Corinthian Christians, you will be asked to apply Paul's lesson to your own lives by reflecting on the ways that our society ascribes status, honor, and prestige. Do we unwittingly bring those habits and values to church too? The group will explore how Paul would respond to some of the ways that we rank and classify each other.

LUTHERAN CONTEXT

Your group will reflect on two important insights developed by Martin Luther from his studies of Scripture. Paul's comments in 1 Corinthians 1:18-25 were the starting point for Martin Luther's meditations on the **theology of the cross.** This might be summed up as the conviction that God is revealed most fully where and when we are least likely to expect to find the divine presence. The death of Jesus on the cross, the ultimate symbol of shame and humiliation in the ancient world, reveals something extraordinary and profound about God's love for humanity. The theology of the cross also points us to those for whom God has a special concern—the foolish, the weak, the low and despised (1 Corinthians 1:27-28)—and has important implications for how we are to treat others. Learners will be asked to explore the implications of the theology of the cross in their own lives.

Luther insisted that **baptism** is God's action even though it is carried out by human hands. Luther's theology of the cross will provide the lens for examining this insight. Is it reasonable to expect God to be present in human activities and in ordinary earthly things like water? Could infant baptism be one of those foolish things that God chooses to do in order to confound the worldly and the wise? Participants will be encouraged to reflect on the meaning of their own baptisms.

DEVOTIONAL CONTEXT

Whose are you? To whom do you belong? In baptism, each one of us is named: "_____, child of God, you have been sealed by the Holy Spirit and marked with the cross of Christ forever" (ELW, p. 231). You belong to God. You are God's. In your devotional reflections on this session, you will lead your learners in a discussion of what it means to belong to God. How does the fact that we have been claimed by God in baptism affect all the other claims that are put on us in our lives? What claims get in the way of our relationship with God? How might we ask God to help us put those claims in their proper place and perspective?

Encourage each participant to spend some time reflecting on the significance of baptism. How might your life be different if you had not been claimed by Christ for God? Conclude with the rite of Thanksgiving for Baptism (ELW, p. 97).

> *Theology of the cross:*
> The idea that God appears in the very last place we would reasonably think to look—in the manger and on the cross. We can discern this theology throughout the Bible (for example, God's choice of Moses, an old man with a speech impediment, to confront Pharaoh; Christ's choice of Paul, a man who had persecuted the early church, to take the gospel to the Gentiles). This theology is also evident in God's special concern for the weak, the foolish, the lowly, and the most vulnerable people on this planet.

> *Baptism:*
> The ritual action of dipping water over a person symbolizing new birth "in Christ." Some of the Corinthian Christians thought that this ritual created a relationship between the baptizer and the one being baptized, similar to the relationship between a parent and child. Paul insists that God is the source of life in Christ; therefore the baptized should boast in the Lord and not their baptizer (1 Corinthians 1:30-31).

SESSION ONE

Facilitator's Prayer

Heavenly Father, source of my life in Christ, thank you for claiming me in my baptism. Thank you for the gift of forgiveness and salvation. Thank you for the gift of your Holy Spirit. Open my heart and mind to the Spirit's calling and enlightening through your Word in Scripture. Open my heart to those who gather with me to study your Word. Open my ears to hear them and my mouth to share your gospel. Amen.

Gather (10-15 minutes)

Check-in

Take time to greet each person and invite learners to introduce themselves to one another.

Pray

Blessed Lord God, you have caused the Holy Scriptures to be written for the nourishment of your people. Grant that we may hear them, read, mark, learn and inwardly digest them, that comforted by your promises, we may embrace and forever hold fast to the hope of eternal life, which you have given us in Jesus Christ, our Savior and Lord. Amen. (ELW, p. 72)

Focus Activity

In one minute or less, write down the names of persons or groups that claim you as theirs.

Tip:
Arrange chairs in a circle around a small table on which you place a bowl and a pitcher of water (you will use these in the thanksgiving for baptism at the end of the session). Have copies of ELW available for the learners. You may wish to encourage learners to wear name tags if anyone is new to your group.

Tip:
Invite participants to pray the opening prayer together out loud as a group.

Tip:
Provide paper and pens or pencils for the learners. As time allows, invite participants (if they are comfortable doing so) to share responses in groups of two or three.

Open Scripture (10-15 minutes)

Ask three volunteers to read in turn 1 Corinthians 1:1-9; 1:10-17; and 1:18-31. As the Bible passage is read, have participants underline words or phrases that catch their attention.

Ask listeners to gravitate toward a single word from the reading that they will later share with the group, along with the reasons that word remained in their hearts and minds.

Read 1 Corinthians 1:1-30.
- What words or phrases caught your attention as you listened to this text?

- What people or situations were called to mind?
- What concerns were raised?

Join the Conversation (25-55 minutes)

Literary Context

1. The first three verses of the session Scripture text make it clear that this is a letter written by the apostle Paul to the congregation he founded in Corinth. This was one of several congregations he established in cities scattered around the eastern end of the Mediterranean Sea. This letter is part of an ongoing long-distance relationship between Paul and members of the Corinthian church involving multiple letters, some of which have not survived (see 1 Corinthians 5:9; 7:1).

- Reading this letter is like listening in on one side of a telephone conversation. Based on what Paul says in 1 Corinthians 1, how would you describe his relationship with the church in Corinth? What seems to be happening in the congregation?
- Reread 1 Corinthians 1:2-9 and 1:26-31 and circle the words that Paul uses to describe the Corinthian congregation and its members. What are the characteristics of the church and its members? What or who is the source of these attributes? To whom do the people belong?

2. Wisdom is an important theme in the first two chapters of 1 Corinthians, where Paul contrasts God's wisdom with worldly wisdom.

- Look again at 1 Corinthians 1:17-31. What is wisdom? What is at the heart and center of God's wisdom, according to Paul?
- List some examples of worldly wisdom that are current in our culture today. How would they measure up against God's wisdom, as defined by Paul?

Historical Context

1. First Corinthians was written about five years after Paul planted the church in Corinth. This means that the first readers were relatively new Christians. They were still learning how to integrate faith with their previously held values, attitudes, and behavior. As first-century Greeks and Romans, they had

Tip:
Participants may find it helpful to have access to a Bible dictionary and/or a theological dictionary.

Tip:
Expand your church library! Throughout this study, a variety of books, videos, and additional resources are recommended. Consider purchasing a copy of items that may be of particular interest to participants and then donating them to the church library when the study is finished.

SESSION ONE

 Bonus Activity:
It will be helpful to better understand Paul's background, call, and work in Corinth. Display a map of Paul's missionary journeys. Form three groups and assign each group a text: Galatians 1:11—2:14, Philippians 3:4-6, Acts 18:1-21. Have the smaller groups share their findings with the large group.

 Tip:
The *Frontline* documentary *From Jesus to Christ: The First Christians* includes several minutes of footage about Paul and Corinth. It is available at www.pbs.org and may be viewed online with a laptop and projector or large-screen monitor. Alternatively, the entire documentary may be purchased online at www.shoppbs.org.

 Tip:
As you prepare for this session, review the differences between Luther's theology of the cross and a theology of glory. A theology of glory conveys the message that being a Christian will make your life better, happier, wealthier, healthier, and/or more successful. A theology of the cross emphasizes God's love and grace in Christ, who claims us as his own even when we feel troubled, poor, and unattractive. For deeper insights, check out the resources listed under "For Further Reading."

 Bonus Activity:
Consider how a "theology of the cross" may be present in the following movies: *Oh God!* (Warner Bros. Pictures, 1977), *Babette's Feast* (Panorama Films A/S, 1988), *The Matrix* (Warner Home Video, 1999), and *Bruce Almighty* (Universal Pictures, 2003). How do these movies challenge popular ideas about God?

 Bonus Activity:
Sing or read the words of the hymn "We Are Baptized in Christ Jesus" (ELW 451), which is based on Romans 6:1-4. Ask participants to reflect on how the cross shapes the lives of the baptized. What does it mean to walk in newness of life?

been raised in a culture that placed a very high value on public honor and prestige deriving from social status. If one was not nobly born, well educated, or influential in society, one could acquire public prestige by associating with those who were. Working for, providing services to, and being seen in the company of high-status persons were ways that one could improve one's public image.

- Reread 1 Corinthians 1:10-16. How are these values evident in the behavior of the Corinthian Christians?
- To learn more about Apollos and Cephas, read Acts 18:24—19:1 and Galatians 1:18—2:14. What attributes of these men might have given them higher status than Paul, in the eyes of some Corinthian Christians?

2. Look at 1 Corinthians 1:26-31 again. According to Paul, what does God think of the Corinthian concern for honor and status among church members?

- What characteristics give church members status and importance today? How would Paul respond to these persons?

Lutheran Context

1. Martin Luther's teaching about the "theology of the cross" states that God comes to us in the very last place a reasonable person would think to look: as a baby sleeping in a manger, as a rough carpenter/healer/teacher from a backwoods region, and as a condemned rebel dying on a Roman cross.

- Reread 1 Corinthians 1:18-25. How does this passage support the theology of the cross?
- According to the theology of the cross, where are we most likely to find God present and actively at work in our communities? What implications does the theology of the cross have for how we ought to treat one another?

2. In the *Large Catechism*, Luther writes, "To be baptized in God's name is to be baptized not by human beings but by God himself. Although it is performed by human hands, it is nevertheless truly God's own act" (*The Book of Concord: The Confessions of the Evangelical Lutheran Church*, ed. Robert Kolb and Timothy J. Wengert, [Fortress Press, 2000]. 457.10).

- How does Luther's theology of the cross help us understand how God is active in human actions involving ordinary things like water?

SESSION ONE

- Consider Luther's claim that baptism is God's act. How does this change the way you think about baptism and what it means in your life?

Devotional Context

1. Look back at the Focus Image for the session. How does that image relate to Paul's message about baptism in 1 Corinthians 1:10-17? How might it resonate with Luther's understanding of baptism? How does it reflect your own experience of baptism?

2. Review the order for Holy Baptism in *Evangelical Lutheran Worship* (pp. 225-31). Reflect on how the words of the service might help us understand whose we are and to whom we belong.

- Draw or describe how you would picture doubt, then do the same for faith. What similarities and differences do you see between doubt and faith?
- Write or say a prayer asking and expecting God to give you the gift of wisdom.

Wrap-up

1. If there are any questions to explore further, write them on chart paper or a whiteboard. Ask for volunteers to do further research to share with the group at the next session.

2. As time allows, circle back to the opening question. Ask for the group to share new insights gained from your time together.

3. Ask learners to share any special prayer requests that they might have for the upcoming week. Encourage participants to pray for each other.

Pray

We give you thanks, O God, that through water and the Holy Spirit you give us new birth, cleanse us from sin, and raise us to eternal life. Stir up in your people the gift of your Holy Spirit: the spirit of wisdom and understanding, the spirit of counsel and might, the spirit of knowledge and the fear of the Lord, the spirit of joy in your presence, both now and forever. Amen. (ELW, p. 237)

Tip:
Be aware of and sensitive to any participants who may not be baptized. Let everyone know that baptism may take place at any point in one's life, from infancy to old age and every age in between. Some participants may not feel comfortable sharing their personal responses; assure everyone that responding to these questions is completely voluntary.

Bonus Activity:
Gather around the baptismal font and give thanks for the gift of baptism, using the rite of Thanksgiving for Baptism (ELW, p. 97). At the end of the rite, each participant may dip his or her fingers into the water and make the sign of the cross upon his or her own forehead in remembrance of baptism.

Tip:
Some learners may feel uncomfortable sharing personal responses. Make it clear that sharing is always voluntary.

Tip:
You may wish to sing the hymn "Baptized in Water" (ELW 456) or another appropriate baptismal hymn.

SESSION ONE

 Tip:
Encourage participants to keep a daily journal for recording their reflections on Homework and Enrichment activities. You may even wish to provide a low-cost journal for each learner.

Extending the Conversation (5 minutes)

Homework

1. Read the next session's Bible text: 1 Corinthians 3:1—4:5.

2. Begin each day by remembering your baptism and reminding yourself that you have been claimed by Christ for God, who is the source of your life and your salvation.

3. Become a "theologian of the cross" who intentionally seeks to be open to God's presence in the ordinary, hidden, and unexpected. Spend some time each day looking and listening for Christ in places where you would not normally expect to see, hear, or experience the divine. You might keep a daily journal in which you record your sightings of this God who is hidden in the ordinary.

Enrichment

1. If you want to read all of 1 and 2 Corinthians during this unit, read the following sections this week.
- Day 1: 1 Corinthians 1:1-17
- Day 2: 1 Corinthians 1:18-25
- Day 3: 1 Corinthians 1:26—2:5
- Day 4: 1 Corinthians 2:6-16
- Day 5: 1 Corinthians 3:1-9
- Day 6: 1 Corinthians 3:10-15
- Day 7: 1 Corinthians 3:16—4:5

2. Learn more about wisdom in the Bible and in the ancient world. You might read Job 28, Proverbs 1–2 and 8–9, or Ecclesiastes in the Bible; or search the Internet for information about ancient philosophers (literally "lovers of wisdom") such as Plato, Aristotle, the Epicureans, and the Stoics.

3. Watch the movie *Romero* (Paulist Productions, 1989) or *Bonhoeffer: Agent of Grace* (Vision Video, 2000). How is God's wisdom evident in these stories?

For Further Reading

Charles B. Cousar, *A Theology of the Cross: The Death of Jesus in the Pauline Letters* (Augsburg Fortress, 1990).

Douglas John Hall, "The Theology of the Cross: A Usable Past." Available at www.elca.org.

From Jesus to Christ: The First Christians. DVD and book available at www.shoppbs.org.

Robert Kolb, "Luther on the Theology of the Cross" *Lutheran Quarterly* 14 (2002): 443-466. Available at www.lutheranquarterly.com (previous issues, Winter 2002).

Martin E. Marty, *Baptism: A User's Guide* (Augsburg Fortress, 2008).

Kirsi Stjerna, *No Greater Jewel: Thinking about Baptism with Luther* (Augsburg Fortress, 2009).

Looking Ahead

1. Read the next session's Bible text: 1 Corinthians 3:1—4:5.

2. Read through the Leader Guide for the next session and mark portions you wish to highlight for the group.

3. Make a checklist of any materials you'll need to do the Bonus Activities.

4. Pray for members of your group during the week.

SESSION TWO

1 Corinthians 3:1—4:5

Leader Session Guide

Focus Statement
We are all servants, laborers working together in God's field and on God's building, the temple. Each one of us is also part of God's field and temple that needs planting, watering, and building up.

Key Verse
For we are God's servants, working together; you are God's field, God's building.... Do you not know that you are God's temple and that God's Spirit dwells in you?
1 Corinthians 3:9, 16

Focus Image

© Hilary Seselja / iStockphoto

What Then Am I?

Session Preparation

Before You Begin . . .

Take a moment to reflect on how you see yourself at this point in your life. Are you a leader or follower, employer or employee, master or servant? Are you mature, wise, and knowledgeable, or perhaps confused, uncertain, and searching for answers? What do you want to be? What do you aspire to be?

Session Instructions

1. Read this Session Guide completely and highlight or underline any portions you wish to emphasize with the group. Note any Bonus Activities you wish to do.

2. If you plan to do any special activities, check to see what materials you'll need, if any.

3. Have extra Bibles on hand in case a member of the group forgets to bring one.

Session Overview

Having learned in the last session that we belong to God, we now ask, "What then am I?" The session Scripture text teaches us that we are infants in faith, like fields that have been planted but need watering, like buildings with foundations but incomplete walls. In the midst of this reality, we are called to be servants laboring together with God to build up each other's faith, and so to build up God's church in the world.

Literary Context

A close reading of this text reveals four key ideas that Paul feels are necessary for healthy faith communities.

First, Paul uses familial language to describe the members of his congregations, referring to them as "brothers and sisters." They all share the same status of being siblings to one another, children of God. Paul also calls them "infants." While this may suggest a parental relationship, it might be more logically consistent to see Paul presenting himself as an older, wiser sibling relating to the baby of the family.

Second, Paul provides a reality check by pointing out to the Corinthian Christians that their behavior demonstrates that they are still **people of the flesh**, merely human, and not the **spiritual people** they think they are and aspire to be.

Third, Paul insists that human leaders, such as apostles, prophets, teachers, pastors, and others, are like servants planting crops or watering what has already been planted, master builders laying foundations or laborers building on top of already-laid foundations. Human leaders in the church are servants and stewards who will be held accountable for their work by God.

Fourth, throughout this letter Paul uses the ancient Greek plural form of the word *you*. So when he says, "You are God's temple," he is addressing the entire congregation as a collective entity. All the baptized together, assembled around Word and Sacrament, are God's temple in which the Holy Spirit dwells. (This idea will be explored in more detail in the next session.)

Participants will be asked to reflect on these ideas as responses to the question, "What then am I?" Do we see ourselves as siblings, as part of a large family consisting of older and younger brothers and sisters? Do we think of ourselves as spiritual people or as people of the flesh, as merely human? Do we see our pastors and/or ourselves as servants and laborers working in someone else's field or construction site? Do we see ourselves as part of a community in which God's Spirit dwells? Why or why not?

Historical Context

Learners will be asked to read the session Scripture text as Paul's presentation of a set of values, attitudes, and practices that are contrary to the worldly wisdom of the first-century Greco-Roman world. Paul replaces the Corinthians' culturally informed view of the church as an arena for competition over status, honor, and prestige with images of cooperative labor. One plants, another waters. One lays the foundation, another constructs the walls, and yet another roofs the building. All work together for a common purpose, motivated and empowered by God, who gives the growth. That being the case, Paul insists that in the church all the glory should be given to God, who is the source of life and growth. Human leaders will be appropriately compensated and rewarded by God in God's time.

Group members will be asked to consider how Paul's values might have changed the way that the Corinthians behaved

People of the flesh:

Persons who lack the gift of God's Spirit, and hence are merely human, closed in on themselves, closed to God and what pleases God, perhaps even in active rebellion against God.

Spiritual people:

Persons who in baptism have received God's Spirit, which opens their hearts and minds to God and what pleases God.

SESSION TWO

toward their leaders and one another. How does Paul's teaching affect the way that we think and act toward our leaders and toward one another? To what extent is Paul's teaching in this area still countercultural? Does our contemporary culture encourage us to see our leaders and ourselves as servants and stewards?

Lutheran Context

Our Lutheran theological heritage provides two important insights that can help participants put the message of 1 Corinthians 3:1—4:5 in perspective.

First, the doctrine of the **priesthood of the baptized** (or priesthood of all believers) asserts that all believers, by virtue of their baptism, share equally in God's mission in the world. All believers are worthy and able to pray for, teach, and minister to one another. This insight enables us to see that whatever Paul says about church leaders also applies to church members. All believers are called to exercise this priesthood in the various circumstances of our lives: in our homes, in the midst of our families, in our workplaces, and in our neighborhoods. Group members will be encouraged to see themselves as God's servants planting, watering, laying foundations, and building up God's mission and ministry in the world.

Second, Luther's insistence that believers are ***simul justus et peccator***—simultaneously saints and sinners—reminds us that the baptized are like sick people in the process of being healed but not whole yet. Or we might use Paul's terms to say that believers are "people of the flesh" in the early stages of becoming "spiritual people." Jealousy and quarrels, growing out of values and practices promoted as worldly wisdom, are symptoms of the sin/sickness/fleshiness that lingers throughout all our lives. Like the Corinthian Christians, we remain "infants in Christ" precisely because we are sinners becoming saints. Participants will reflect on how being mindful of this can keep us focused on mission.

Devotional Context

In baptism we have been claimed by God. In light of the reality that we belong to God, that we are God's, we ask, "What then am I?" First Corinthians 3:1—4:5 provides a number of possible answers: a brother or sister in Christ, an infant in Christ, a servant who plants, a servant who waters, a master builder laying foundations, a laborer building up from previously laid foundations, a servant of Christ, and a steward of God's

---

? *Priesthood of the baptized*:

The teaching based in 1 Peter 2:9 that all baptized believers without distinction are called to the ministry of Word and Sacrament. Each person exercises this ministry in his or her specific vocation. The task of ordained pastors is to equip the baptized for ministry in their vocations in the home, the workplace, and the larger community.

? *Simul justus et peccator*:

A Latin phrase that is often rendered "simultaneously saint and sinner" and gets at the heart of Luther's conviction that the baptized are like sick people in the care of a physician engaged in healing them. The baptized are saints in hope and anticipation of the healing that is under way.

mysteries. In your devotional reflections on this session, you will lead learners in a discussion that explores the priesthood of the baptized as experienced in their own lives.

Give group members time to recall their own journeys of faith, identifying the persons who were instrumental in planting, nourishing, and nurturing their commitment to Christ and the church. Encourage learners to share their stories.

Lead participants through a review of the mission and ministries that are ongoing in your congregation. The goal here is to see that ministry is not just something that the pastor does, but that there are many people involved in many aspects of your congregation's ministry.

Encourage learners to see that many of the things that they do in daily life outside the church are ministry too.

Facilitator's Prayer

Gracious God, who claimed me in baptism, thank you for _____ , your servants who have nurtured and nourished my faith. Inspire my speaking and listening today, so that I too may be your faithful servant planting, watering, and building up faith in others. Praise to you, the source of life and salvation, for giving us growth in our faith, discipleship, and daily ministries. Amen.

Gather (10-15 minutes)

Check-in

Invite learners to share completed homework or any new thoughts or insights about the last session. Be ready to give a brief recap of that session if necessary.

Pray

Gracious and holy God, give us diligence to seek you, wisdom to perceive you, and patience to wait for you. Grant us, O God, a mind to meditate on you; eyes to behold you; ears to listen for your word; a heart to love you; and a life to proclaim you; through the power of the Spirit of Jesus Christ, our Savior and Lord. Amen. (ELW, p. 76)

Tip:
Encourage participants to wear name tags, especially if there are any learners who are new to your group or could benefit from visual reminders of one another's names.

Tip:
Invite participants to pray the opening prayer together out loud as a group.

Session 2: 1 Corinthians 3:1—4:5

SESSION TWO

 Tip:
Have learners share responses to the Focus Image in groups of two or three.

Focus Activity

Look at the Focus Image and think about the people involved in your growth in faith. Who has helped to plant the seeds, water and nurture the soil, and so on?

Open Scripture (10-15 minutes)

Ask participants to close their eyes and just listen to the passage as it is read slowly and carefully by one person. Invite them to share what images and/or feelings the text evokes.

Ask three volunteers to read in turn 1 Corinthians 3:1-9; 3:10-20; and 3:21—4:5, with a brief pause between each section. Have participants identify the image and tone that dominate each section.

Read 1 Corinthians 3:1—4:5.
- What words or phrases caught your attention as you listened to this text?
- How would you describe the tone of this passage? How does it make you feel?
- What issues were raised?

Join the Conversation (25-55 minutes)

Literary Context

1. Human beings label each other and call each other names (for example, darling or jerk) as a way of evaluating each other positively or negatively. In his desire to correct the behavior of church members, Paul attaches a number of labels to them.
- Reread 1 Corinthians 3:1-4 and circle or underline the different ways that Paul refers to the Corinthian Christians. What effect would these labels have on the hearers? What effect would these labels have on you if they came from a respected mentor?

2. A metaphor is a figure of speech that transfers meanings from one concept to another through comparison or resemblance (for example, God's Word is a lamp). In 1 Corinthians 3:5—4:1, Paul uses a number of metaphors to clarify the role of church leaders.
- Identify the metaphors in this text and the areas of everyday life from which Paul draws them.

Tip:
Participants may find it helpful to have access to a Bible dictionary and/or a theological dictionary.

 Bonus Activity:
In 1 Corinthians 3:19-20 Paul cautions the Corinthian Christians not to rely too heavily on the wisdom of this world. He supports his contention that worldly wisdom is foolishness with God by referring to Job 5:12-13 and Psalm 94:11. Look up these passages. What do they mean in their original literary context? Does Paul use them appropriately?

22 1, 2 Corinthians Leader Guide

- How well do these metaphors help you respond to the question, "What then am I?" How well do they help you understand your role in the life of your congregation? What other metaphors would you use?

3. In ancient Greek, as in many modern languages, there were different words for "you" (singular) and "you" (plural). Throughout Paul's letter to the Corinthians, he uses the plural form of the word.
- How does this affect the meaning of 1 Corinthians 3:16-17? What is Paul saying about the church as a whole?
- What evidence do you see today that the Holy Spirit resides in the church—the assembly of the baptized?

Historical Context

1. In session 1, we learned that ancient Greek and Roman societies were very status conscious, giving much honor and prestige to those who were nobly born, well educated, and holders of important public offices. Ordinary people competed for social status by boasting of their connections to such prestigious persons. These values and attitudes were reflected in the Corinthian church as cliques formed around leaders, and members argued over the relative merits and status of the persons who had been instrumental in bringing them to faith and/or baptizing them. The result was "jealousy and quarreling" (1 Corinthians 3:3).
- Identify who, according to Paul, should get the credit for bringing the Corinthians to faith, baptizing them, and building up their congregation.
- Reread 1 Corinthians 3:3; 3:12-15; and 4:3-5. Discuss how church leaders will be evaluated and by whom. How would Paul's advice affect the way the Corinthian Christians treat their leaders and each other?

2. Consider to what extent Paul's teaching on this subject is still countercultural—still contrary to the wisdom of this world (3:18-19). Discuss whether our contemporary values encourage us to see our leaders and ourselves as servants and stewards.

Lutheran Context

1. Lutheran theology upholds the "priesthood of the baptized," sometimes called the "priesthood of all believers." As Martin Luther explained, all who are baptized and believe in Christ are priests as stated in 1 Peter 2:9, and so are worthy to pray for, teach, and minister to one another, even if all do not do so

Bonus Activity:
What "Day" is Paul referring to in 1 Corinthians 3:13? Have participants take a quick look through the following passages to explore what this is all about: Isaiah 13:6-9; Joel 2:1-2; Amos 5:18-20; Zephaniah 1:7-18; 1 Thessalonians 4:13—5:11; and 2 Thessalonians 2:1-12.

Tip:
It might be helpful to review the Historical Context in session 1.

Bonus Activity:
In the Greco-Roman world, stewards were managerial slaves responsible for overseeing the household, business, and political affairs of their masters. When Paul calls himself a steward of God's mysteries (4:1-5), what is he saying? Read other passages that mention stewards: Luke 12:41-48 and 16:1-8; Romans 16:23; Galatians 4:2; Titus 1:7; and 1 Peter 4:10-11. Based on these texts, identify the basic elements of stewardship.

Bonus Activity:
List ways that your congregation encourages you to see leaders and members as servants and stewards.

SESSION TWO

Tip:
If you decide to do the bonus activities, make sure each member of the study group has a copy of *Evangelical Lutheran Worship*.

Bonus Activity:
To explore how deeply the concept of the priesthood of the baptized is embedded in Lutheran faith and life, take a look at the "Topical Index of Hymns" in *Evangelical Lutheran Worship* (pp. 1178–1188). How many of the topics listed relate to the priesthood of all believers or ministry in daily life? Think about your favorite hymns. How many of them lift up elements of these teachings?

Bonus Activity:
Lutheran worship seeks to keep us mindful of the reality of what we are. Review the order for Confession and Forgiveness on pages 94–96 in *Evangelical Lutheran Worship*. How do the words of this rite connect with and reflect the biblical and theological insight that we are people of flesh/sinners in the process of becoming spiritual people/saints?

Tip:
Give participants some time to work through the questions in this section on their own before inviting them to share their thoughts with a few others or the large group.

Bonus Activity:
For more ideas on celebrating the priesthood of the baptized, take a look at "Equipping and Encouraging Laity" by Nelvin L. Vos and Melvin G. George in *Lutheran Partners* 18, no. 3 (May/June 2002), available at http://archive.elca.org/lutheranpartners/archives/eqiplait.html.

publicly as ordained ministers ("The Freedom of a Christian" [1520], reprinted in *Martin Luther's Basic Theological Writings*, 2nd ed., ed. Timothy F. Lull [Augsburg Fortress, 2005], 398–400).

- Reread 1 Corinthians 3:5-15, replacing the names Apollos and Paul with your own names. As members of the priesthood of the baptized, what are you being called to do? What tasks do you or can you perform in God's field, in God's temple?

2. The Latin phrase *simul justus et peccator* sums up Martin Luther's view of the Christian as a person who is "simultaneously saint and sinner." This means that the baptized are like sick people who are in the care of a physician who is at work healing them. The baptized are saints in the hope and to the extent that healing is taking place.

- List the words and phrases Paul uses in 1 Corinthians 3:1-4 to convey the same idea as "simultaneously saint and sinner." How does Paul's language help us understand Luther's theological point? How does Luther's language help us understand Paul's point?
- Why do Christians, past and present, experience quarrels and divisions? How might Paul's advice in the rest of the session Scripture text help us to refocus on what is really important?

Devotional Context

1. Think about your journey of faith and the persons who have nurtured and nourished your faith. Identify and name the persons who laid the foundations of your faith, planted it, watered it, and so on.

2. Review the mission of your congregation. Identify, if you can, those who planted the congregation, the charter members, and those who built on the foundations that these people laid. Who is doing ministry in your congregation today? How many people in your congregation are engaged in this ministry?

3. Reflect on your own daily life and your occupation, community involvement, and activities. Would you call any of this ministry? Why or why not? If you went through your daily routine mindful that you were exercising the priesthood of the baptized, how might that affect what you do and how you do it?

SESSION TWO

Wrap-up

1. If there are any questions to explore further, write them on chart paper or a whiteboard. Ask for volunteers to do further research to share with the group at the next session.

2. Invite participants to share the most surprising thing they have learned about how the Bible and Lutheran theology answer the question, "What then am I?"

Pray

Gracious God, we thank you for raising up committed servants like Paul and Apollos, who planted and watered the faith of the first Christians. We thank you for all men and women through the ages who have been faithful stewards of the good news. We thank you especially for those men and women who have nurtured and nourished our faith. Empower us to be faithful servants and stewards of your gospel and your grace. In Jesus' name we pray. Amen.

Extending the Conversation (5 minutes)

Homework

1. Read the next session's Bible text: 1 Corinthians 6:12-20 and 10:23-33.

2. In your prayers this week, thank God for the persons who were instrumental in nurturing your faith. If possible, call or write these persons and tell them what a difference they have made in your life.

3. Exercise your priesthood of the baptized by doing one or more of the following: praying for each other and anyone you feel is in special need; personally forgiving someone who has hurt or offended you (if you can't do this in person, consider writing a letter—it doesn't matter if they don't respond); offering to teach or help with Sunday school or another children's or youth ministry; becoming a mentor to a young person in your congregation; sharing your faith story with a child (in person or in writing); volunteering at a homeless shelter, food pantry, or other agency; visiting the sick or shut-in; helping to keep your community clean and safe; or becoming more aware of and/or engaged in local issues.

Tip:
Some participants may not be comfortable sharing personal responses. Make it clear that sharing is always voluntary.

Tip:
Invite participants to pray together out loud and, if they wish, to lift up any special prayer requests that may have arisen from this session or that they may have on their hearts.

Tip:
Encourage learners to continue journaling about their thoughts and reflections on each session and their Homework and Enrichment activities.

SESSION TWO

Enrichment

1. If you want to read all of 1 and 2 Corinthians during this unit, read the following sections this week.
- Day 1: 1 Corinthians 3:1-23
- Day 2: 1 Corinthians 4:1-20
- Day 3: 1 Corinthians 5:1—6:20
- Day 4: 1 Corinthians 7:1-39
- Day 5: 1 Corinthians 8:1-13
- Day 6: 1 Corinthians 9:1-27
- Day 7: 1 Corinthians 10:1—11:1

2. To understand current Lutheran thinking on the priesthood of the baptized, visit the Web site of the Evangelical Lutheran Church in America (www.elca.org). Click on "Growing in Faith," "Vocation," and then "Ministry in Daily Life." Explore the various articles on that page, especially those under "Ministry in Daily Life Theology."

3. Watch the movie *Babette's Feast* (Panorama Films A/S, 1988) or *Chocolat* (Miramax Films, 2000). How is the reality that humans are *simul justus et peccator* (simultaneously saints and sinners) depicted and played out in these films?

For Further Reading

Dave Daubert and Tana Kjos, with Kelly A. Fryer, *Reclaiming the "V" Word: Renewing Life at Its Vocational Core* (Augsburg Fortress, 2009).

Frank G. Honeycutt, *Sanctified Living: More Than Grace and Forgiveness* (Augsburg Fortress, 2008).

Uwe Siemon-Netto, "Work Is Our Mission," *Christianity Today*, November 2007, 30-32.

Looking Ahead

1. Read the next session's Bible text: 1 Corinthians 6:12-20 and 10:23-33.

2. Read through the Leader Guide for the next session and mark portions you wish to highlight for the group.

3. Make a checklist of any materials you'll need to do the Bonus Activities.

4. Pray for members of your group during the week.

SESSION THREE

1 Corinthians 6:12-20; 10:23-33

Leader Session Guide

Focus Statement

Freedom in Christ is not permission for selfish indulgence. Freedom in Christ liberates us for service to the other.

Key Verse

So, whether you eat or drink, or whatever you do, do everything for the glory of God. 1 Corinthians 10:31

Focus Image

© PeskyMonkey / iStockphoto

It's Not All about Me?

Session Preparation

Before You Begin . . .

Take a moment to reflect on what others see and hear when they are with you. Do they see a magnet drawing all attention to itself or a sign pointing the way for others? Do your actions say, "It's all about me," or "I'm here to make a difference for you"? Is your conversation all about "I-me-my" or is it equal parts listening to and building up the other? Who gets the glory?

Session Instructions

1. Read this Session Guide completely and highlight or underline any portions you wish to emphasize with the group. Note any Bonus Activities you wish to do.

2. If you plan to do any special activities, check to see what materials you'll need, if any.

3. Have extra Bibles on hand in case a member of the group forgets to bring one.

Session Overview

In baptism we are claimed by Jesus Christ, declared precious children of God, and filled with the Holy Spirit. We know that God loves us and will forgive us when we mess up. But does that mean we can do anything and everything we want? In this session we learn that following Jesus is not all about me, but about honoring ourselves, the people around us, and the church, which is the body of Christ.

LITERARY CONTEXT

In the session Scripture texts and related passages in 1 Corinthians, Paul deals with two different behavior problems in the Corinthian church:

- Sexual impropriety in the form of an incestuous relationship (5:1-8) and visiting prostitutes (6:12-20).
- Eating meat sacrificed to idols, both in private and in public settings (8:1-13 and 10:14-33). Some church members had even been seen eating in pagan temples (8:10).

SESSION THREE

Paul's responses in 6:12-20 and 10:23-33 are structurally similar. He quotes the slogans that some Corinthian believers are using to justify their behavior: "All things are lawful for me" (6:12; 10:23). Paul's responses are given in the form of "yes, but..." statements. In this way he both affirms and corrects his audience's understanding by asking them to assess whether these behaviors are beneficial, enslaving, or upbuilding. Paul's point is that some believers are too narrowly focused on their own desires and pleasure. For them, it's all about me.

Paul asserts two things in his responses:

- Sexual impropriety is a sin against the body itself (6:18). Because the individual's physical body is a member of Christ who is embodied in the church, sexual impropriety harms both the individual and the church.
- Believers cannot eat meat sacrificed to idols in any worship setting (10:14-22). Meat sold in the marketplace is neutral (10:25), but when dining in private, believers must take into account the consciences of fellow diners (believers and unbelievers alike).

Paul's point is that for believers, it's never all about me. What we do affects others; therefore, whatever we do should be for God's glory (10:31).

HISTORICAL CONTEXT

The congregation in Corinth consisted of new believers raised with ancient Greco-Roman values and ideas. Philosophers taught that the body was a tomb for the soul, and at best it was irrelevant for spiritual development. In opposition to this view, Paul boldly claims that not only are our spirits united with Christ, but so too are our bodies. Physical activities have spiritual consequences.

Church members from different social or ethnic backgrounds had different views on many issues including if, when, and where it was appropriate to eat meat or other foods offered to idols.

- The philosophically educated minority argued that since idols were not real, no spiritual harm came of eating food offered to them (8:1-6). Attendance at sacrifices was part of the official duties of some church members like Erastus the city treasurer (Romans 16:23; Acts 19:22).
- The majority of people believed that idols represented powerful ***daimons***. Eating food offered to them in sacrificial rituals was believed to establish a partnership or communion of

> **? Daimons:**
> The Greek word *daimōns*, from which we derive the word *demons*, originally referred to powerful invisible spirits that, according to their temperaments, either protected or afflicted humans. Greek-speaking Jews like Paul regarded all idols, alien gods, and evil spirits as daimons.

protection. Greeks and Romans normally ate and worshipped at the tables of many different deities, but Jews sacrificed only at the temple in Jerusalem. In trying to resolve this issue for the early church, Paul seeks answers in his Jewish scriptural heritage (10:18-22).

While Paul at first appears to affirm the arguments of the elite (8:1-6), in the end he asks them to modify their behavior, out of respect for the consciences of fellow believers and others whose faith may be threatened by such practices (8:7-13; 10:23-33).

Lutheran Context

"Cheap grace" accepts and excuses sin by claiming that God loves me just as I am, knows I'm doing the best I can, and so will forgive me. Cheap grace permits the believer to replace discipleship (walking in the footsteps of Jesus) with the pursuit of worldly success and happiness. Here is what can happen when cheap grace is taken to the extreme:

- cheap grace = God will forgive anything I do because God loves me

  can become

- **libertinism** = God loves me, so therefore God is okay with everything I do

In contrast to cheap grace, God's grace is costly. God's grace justifies, or accepts and forgives, sinners because of what Christ has done for us (the "price" that Paul refers to in 6:20), as a prelude to transforming us through faith and other spiritual gifts for vocation and service in the priesthood of the baptized.

Conscience is a compound word made up of two Latin words: *con* = together, and *scire* = to know. Conscience involves knowing together with others. We learn what is right and wrong from our parents, siblings, friends, teachers, pastors, and others with whom we interact closely. A mature conscience develops through correction, dialogue, study, and reflection until it becomes an integral part of who we are, guiding how we behave. Because we are sinners, our conscience is never perfect; it can lead us astray. Yet our conscience is so central to our identity that it can be psychologically and spiritually dangerous to act against it. Not surprisingly, Paul cautions us against violating another's conscience.

> *Cheap grace:*
> The concept defined by Dietrich Bonhoeffer as "the justification of sin without the justification of the sinner." Cheap grace accepts and excuses sin as normal and unavoidable and forgiven by God. It is the opposite of the Lutheran doctrine of "justification by grace through faith for Christ's sake unto good works," which teaches that God accepts sinners for Christ's sake and transforms them through faith and other spiritual gifts for service to the world.

> *Libertinism:*
> The belief that individual conscience, apart from social consequences, is the only valid authority for ethical conduct. It is often associated with a self-centered and indulgent lifestyle involving sexual promiscuity and other "works of the flesh" (see Galatians 5:19-21).

SESSION THREE

DEVOTIONAL CONTEXT

In this portion of the session, encourage participants to think seriously about how the session Scripture texts connect with our lives today.

- Perhaps group members are familiar with Christians who in the past or still today look upon dancing or playing cards as behavior inappropriate for believers and unacceptable in a church. Participants are asked to reflect on whether there are other activities that violate the sanctity of our bodies. If we take seriously Paul's claim that our bodies are members of Christ (temples for the Holy Spirit), how should we treat our bodies? What aspects of our daily lives would change?

- The group is asked to try to identify some widespread contemporary cultural practices that might conflict with following Jesus. Have participants ever run into some attitude, value, or activity accepted by friends and family, employers or coworkers, neighbors or community leaders that violates Christian principles? How do we handle situations like that? Where do we turn for guidance and direction?

- Have participants consider whether they have ever refrained from doing something that they were convinced was absolutely acceptable because it would offend someone else's conscience or sensibilities. How did this feel?

Facilitator's Prayer

Holy God, holy and immortal, I praise you. It's not all about me. Help me to use my body and mind in ways that bring glory and honor to you. May my words and actions show the world that you truly are gracious and merciful, slow to anger and abounding in steadfast love. Be with us as we gather around your Word. In Jesus' name I pray. Amen.

Gather (10-15 minutes)

Check-in

Invite learners to share completed homework or any new thoughts or insights about the last session. Be ready to give a brief recap of that session if necessary.

SESSION THREE

Pray

Almighty God, by our baptism into the death and resurrection of your Son, Jesus Christ, you turn us from the old life of sin. Grant that we who are reborn to new life in him may live in righteousness and holiness all our days, through your Son, Jesus Christ our Lord. Amen. (ELW, p. 86).

Focus Activity

Take a few minutes to look at the Focus Image. Where have you encountered self-centered attitudes or actions recently? How did this impact your life? How did you respond? Reflect on how your self-centered attitudes or actions have affected the people you live and work with, their responses, and the end result for your relationships.

Tip:
Since this activity may involve both accusation and self-disclosure, group members may be more comfortable approaching this as a silent meditation with opportunity for journaling. Make sure everyone has paper and pencils or pens.

Open Scripture (10-15 minutes)

Do a dramatic reading. Have someone play "Paul" and read the sections of 6:12; 6:13; and 10:23 that are not within quotation marks, plus all the other verses. The rest of the group can represent the Corinthian elites by reading the statements within quotation marks in 6:12; 6:13; and 10:23. (Additional roles might be assigned for the quotations from "The Word" in 6:16 and 10:26, and for the unbelieving host's quotation in 10:28.)

Ask participants to close their eyes and just listen to each passage as it is read slowly, but with careful attention to the text, by one person. Be prepared to identify the tone of these texts. Are they more like teaching or preaching?

Read 1 Corinthians 6:12-20 and 10:23-33.
- What words or phrases caught your attention?
- Was there anything surprising or troubling?
- What questions do these texts raise for you?

SESSION THREE

 Tip:
Create two small groups; one group should focus on 5:1-8 and 6:12-20, while the other concentrates on 8:1-13 and 10:14-33. A recorder for each group should write their responses and reflections on chart paper or a whiteboard for sharing with the whole group.

Bonus Activity:
In 1 Corinthians 6:16 Paul quotes Genesis 2:24. Have participants look up and read Genesis 2:18-25. How does this text support Paul's argument about what happens when a man visits a prostitute?

Bonus Activity:
In 1 Corinthians 10:26 Paul quotes Psalm 24:1. Have participants look up and read this text. How does it support Paul's argument about what is sold in the meat market? During the time Paul was writing to the Corinthians, other New Testament texts had not been written yet. To see how later writers addressed issues related to food, look up Mark 7:1-23 and Acts 10:1-15. What authorities are appealed to in these texts?

 Tip:
It may be beneficial to continue working in two small groups through this context as well. Make sure that there is time for each working group to share insights with the large group.

 Bonus Activity:
For background information on the Corinthians' debate about the body, download "Two Views of Body and Soul" by Kalman J. Kaplan, available at http://www.juf.org/news/world.aspx?id=15852. Ask participants to read this short article together with Genesis 2:4-7, and reflect on the differences between the Greek view of the body and the biblical view promoted by Judaism and Christianity.

Join the Conversation (25-55 minutes)

Literary Context

1. Both 1 Corinthians 6:12-20 and 10:23-33 begin the same way: Paul quotes slogans used by some of the Corinthian church members. Write down the slogans quoted in 6:12 and 10:23. What do you think the Corinthian Christians meant by these slogans? What behaviors could they have been trying to rationalize? (See 5:1-8; 6:12-20; 8:1-13; and 10:14-33.)

2. Now write down Paul's responses to these slogans (again in 6:12 and 10:23). Discuss whether Paul agrees or disagrees with the Corinthian Christians. What values does he appear to be lifting up? Who should benefit and not be dominated by anything (6:12-20)? Who should benefit and be built up by things that church members do (10:23-33)?

3. Identify the guiding principle for Christian behavior, according to Paul. (See 6:20 and 10:31.)

Historical Context

1. Some ancient Greek philosophies described the body as a prison or tomb to be overcome, disciplined, or ignored. Some elite church members were visiting prostitutes, justifying their behavior as bodily activity, like eating, that had no spiritual effects (6:13). Thinking they were already spiritual people (3:1) free from bodily concerns led them to *libertinism*, the idea that anything and everything was permissible for them.

- Reread 1 Corinthians 6:12-20. Discuss Paul's understanding of the relationship between body and spirit, how one affects the other, and to whom our bodies belong.

2. The majority of people in the ancient world believed that pollution, disease, and misfortune were caused by invisible spiritual forces called *daimons*. Certain rituals were thought to ward off these negative forces and gain the favor of protective spirits or gods. These rituals often included animal sacrifices. The meat from sacrifices was eaten by worshippers in temples, taken home for celebratory meals, and sold in the marketplace. Sacrifices were thus the source of almost all available meat, which was almost always eaten in the context of worship or family celebration. Elite members of the church were educated in Greco-Roman philosophical traditions, which taught that daimons were not real, and so ritual interaction with them

was just social convention without any spiritual or moral implications.

- Reread 1 Corinthians 8:1-13; 10:14-22; and 10:23—11:1 and note which group Paul seems to agree with. Which group is being asked to modify its behavior? Why?

Lutheran Context

1. In his book *The Cost of Discipleship* (first published in German in 1937; Simon & Schuster, 1996), Dietrich Bonhoeffer describes cheap grace as "the justification of sin without the justification of the sinner." Cheap grace says that God loves us just as we are and so nothing needs to change in our lives. Cheap grace results in a secularized Christianity indistinguishable from the wider culture, in which discipleship is replaced by a program focusing on personal success and happiness.

- Compare the libertinism of elites in the Corinthian church with the concept of cheap grace. Now consider Paul's comment in 1 Corinthians 6:20. Is God's grace free? Who pays the price? What does Paul suggest as an appropriate response on our part?
- Think back to last session's discussion of the priesthood of the baptized. How is the idea of cheap grace at odds with our baptismal calling to the priesthood of the baptized?

2. First Corinthians 8–10 is part of the biblical basis for Lutheran theological reflection on the importance of "the bound conscience." Reread 1 Corinthians 8:7-13 and 10:23-30. What does Paul say here about respecting the conscience of the other? Why is this important, according to Paul?

- Notice that God is at work in both kingdoms, in different ways. What are some other similarities or differences between the two kingdoms?

Devotional Context

1. Paul describes how visiting prostitutes negatively affects both the individual bodies of believers ("your bodies," 6:15-18), and the body of the church in which God's Spirit dwells ("your body," 6:19-20; see also 3:16). What physical activities have been, or perhaps still are, regarded as inappropriate or destructive for individual believers and for the church as a whole? What is the relationship between our behavior as individuals and our behavior as Christians?

Bonus Activity:
What was the point of ancient sacrifice rituals? Explore this question by doing one or more of the following activities:

- If available, use a computer with a large monitor or projector and screen to visit http://inside.bard.edu/academic/specialproj/ritual/Rituals/Burkert/00.html for an illustrated walk-through of Greek sacrifice ritual.
- Read Genesis 4:1-7, the first mention of animal sacrifice in the Bible.
- Look at some of the more detailed instructions for various kinds of offerings recorded in Leviticus 1–7.

Tip:
If you decide to do the bonus activities, make sure each member of the study group has a copy of *Evangelical Lutheran Worship*.

Bonus Activity:
Hymns 587–598 in ELW focus on "Grace, Faith." Have participants look over a selection of these hymns. Do the words of the hymns support the notion of cheap grace? Could they be interpreted in this way?

Bonus Activity:
Hymns 796–818 in ELW highlight "Commitment, Discipleship." Have participants look over a selection of these hymns. What seems to be the common thread here?

Tip:
It may be more effective to have participants return to the two working groups for this section. Make sure that there is sufficient time to share insights with the large group.

Bonus Activity:
Read Psalm 51 from ELW responsively (one small group reading the odd-numbered verses, the other responding with the even-numbered verses), as a prayer of confession and petition for cleansing.

SESSION THREE

2. In first-century Corinth eating meat that came from pagan sacrifices was a problem because it was such a widespread cultural practice that it was almost impossible to avoid. It raised questions about Christian identity. How far could a Christian go along with these practices and still be a Christian?

- Are there any similar issues in our contemporary cultural context? Consider the following possibilities: Is being a faithful disciple of Jesus Christ always compatible with fitting in comfortably with your peer group? Being a good employee? Being a good citizen?

Wrap-up

1. If there are any questions to explore further, write them on chart paper or a whiteboard. Ask for volunteers to do further research to share with the group at the next session.

2. Invite participants to share the most meaningful thing that they learned in this session.

3. Explain and assign any homework for the coming week.

Pray

Create in me a clean heart, O God, and put a new and right spirit within me. Keep me always mindful, Lord, that I am yours—body, mind, and soul; that your Spirit dwells in me and in the people around me. Help me remember that my behavior affects all those people for good or ill. May my words and my actions be instruments of your love and grace. In Jesus' name I pray. Amen.

Extending the Conversation (5 minutes)

Homework

1. Read the next session's Bible text: 1 Corinthians 12:1-31.

2. Spend some time each day reflecting on the session title, "It's Not All about Me?" and/or the Focus Image. Write in a journal about situations where it was or might be helpful for you to remember "It's not all about me." Paul claims that our words and actions affect others around us and reflect on our claim to be Christians. How does being mindful of this affect the way you behave?

3. How prevalent is "cheap grace" in contemporary Christian messages? Take time to scrutinize the content of Christian radio

Tip: Some participants may not be comfortable sharing personal information. Make it clear that sharing is always voluntary.

Tip: You may substitute the Bonus Activity from the Devotional Context for this prayer, if you choose.

Tip: Encourage learners to continue journaling about their thoughts and reflections on each session and their Homework and Enrichment activities.

or television messages, the words and lyrics of your favorite hymns and Christian music, your usual devotional materials or other Christian books you are reading, and Christian Web sites. Consider reporting back to the group on what you find.

Enrichment

1. If you want to read all of 1 and 2 Corinthians during this unit, read the following sections this week.
- Day 1: 1 Corinthians 10:1-22
- Day 2: 1 Corinthians 10:23—11:1
- Day 3: 1 Corinthians 11:2-16
- Day 4: 1 Corinthians 11:17-22
- Day 5: 1 Corinthians 11:23-34
- Day 6: 1 Corinthians 12:1-11
- Day 7: 1 Corinthians 12:12-31

2. Learn more about Dietrich Bonhoeffer—the man, his life, and his theology—by viewing one of these films: *Bonhoeffer: Agent of Grace* (Vision Video, 2000) or *Bonhoeffer: Pastor, Pacifist, Nazi Resister* (First Run Features, 2003).

3. To learn more about the Lutheran concept of the "bound conscience," visit www.elca.org and read the following articles: "FAQs on Bound Conscience," "Remarks Concerning 'Bound Conscience' Presented to the 2009 Churchwide Assembly by the Rev. Dr. Timothy J. Wengert," and "Reflections on the Bound Conscience in Lutheran Theology" by Timothy J. Wengert.

For Further Reading

Renate Bethge, *Dietrich Bonhoeffer: A Brief Life* (Fortress, 2004).

Dietrich Bonhoeffer, *The Cost of Discipleship* (first published in German in 1937; Simon & Schuster, 1996).

Looking Ahead

1. Read the next session's Bible text: 1 Corinthians 12:1-31.

2. Read through the Leader Guide for the next session and mark portions you wish to highlight for the group.

3. Make a checklist of any materials you'll need to do the Bonus Activities.

4. Pray for members of your group during the week.

SESSION FOUR

1 Corinthians 12:1-31

Leader Session Guide

Focus Statement
The Holy Spirit gives each person a gift that is indispensable to the body of Christ.

Key Verse
On the contrary, the members of the body that seem to be weaker are indispensable, and those members of the body that we think less honorable we clothe with greater honor, and our less respectable members are treated with greater respect. 1 Corinthians 12:22-23

Focus Image

© Beata Beckla / iStockphoto

Pneumatika:
Literally means phenomena induced by the Spirit, but is usually translated as "spiritual gifts."

What Am I Good For?

Session Preparation

Before You Begin...

Take a moment to reflect on people you honor and respect. What is it about them that makes them honorable and respected in your eyes? How do you let them know what they are good for? Who shows you honor and respect? Why? How do they let you know what you are good for?

Session Instructions

1. Read this Session Guide completely and highlight or underline any portions you wish to emphasize with the group. Note any Bonus Activities you wish to do.

2. If you plan to do any special activities, check to see what materials you'll need, if any.

3. Have extra Bibles on hand in case a member of the group forgets to bring one.

Session Overview

In 1 Corinthians 12 we learn that God's Spirit empowers us to commit our lives to Jesus as our Lord, equips and energizes us with spiritual gifts for the common good, and makes us part of the body of Christ. Regardless of our ethnicity, social status, abilities, and needs, we are all indispensable members of Christ's body, suffering and rejoicing together with one another along life's way.

HISTORICAL CONTEXT

In 1 Corinthians 12–14 Paul deals with the topic of **pneumatika** in response to the assertions of some church members that speaking in tongues demonstrated a higher spiritual status. Like many ancient peoples, they believed that gods and daimons and other spiritual beings could possess or take control of a person's body and mind, causing them to see and/or hear divine mysteries, and to experience **glossolalia** and other Spirit-induced behaviors. Given their preoccupation with prestige and honor, it is no surprise that some Corinthian Christians wanted to rank the various **pneumatika** manifested in the church.

Paul corrects these Corinthian Christians by insisting that genuinely God-inspired speech and activities always confess and demonstrate that Jesus is Lord (1 Corinthians 12:3) and promote the common good (12:7). He then reframes their understanding of the church by appealing to a widely recognized ancient metaphor: society is a like a body. In Greco-Roman political speeches the body (in this case, society) was presented as a hierarchically ranked set of parts, all obeying the head. In stark contrast, Paul emphasizes that in the church all members are necessary; indeed the weaker, less honorable, less respectable members are indispensable and must be treated with a dignity the world refuses to show them. Paul consistently makes the point that knowledge, power, and authority are to be used for the benefit of others, not wielded over them.

Glossolalia:
Speaking in tongues, specifically ecstatic utterances of unintelligible sounds produced by individuals in a state of altered consciousness.

LITERARY CONTEXT

Paul explains that in the church *pneumatika* take the form of **charismata** (individual gifts or graces), **diakonia** (service-oriented ministries), and **energemata** (energizing or inspiring activities). Participants will be asked to organize Paul's lists in 12:8-10 and 12:28 according to these categories. There are no absolute, hard and fast answers here. Faith, knowledge, and wisdom seem to be gifts/graces of individual persons. Healing clearly is a service-oriented ministry. Some *pneumatika* may fit in more than one category. Prophecy, for instance, may be both an energizing/inspiring activity and a service-oriented ministry (see 1 Corinthians 14:3). Apostles, prophets, and teachers are ministers serving the church, but do so because of individual gifts/graces they have received. Let participants draw their own conclusions.

Charismata:
Spiritual gifts or graces given to the individual believer by God through the Holy Spirit.

Diakonia:
A ministry of serving others, to which believers are called by God through the Holy Spirit.

Energemata:
Energizing or inspiring activities prompted by the Holy Spirit.

Reading 1 Corinthians 14:1-25 will help learners understand the differences between prophecy and glossolalia, and connect these gifts with the life of the church today. Prophecy as described by Paul is not about foretelling the future, but is inspired preaching that builds up, encourages, and consoles believers (14:3) and admonishes unbelievers (14:24-25). Participants may or may not be familiar with glossolalia, which is practiced in some Christian groups, especially in Pentecostal churches. Whatever the reactions and feelings about glossolalia among members of your group, Paul's point in 1 Corinthians 14 is clear: speaking in tongues is not as helpful as the gift of prophecy in building up the church.

SESSION FOUR

LUTHERAN CONTEXT

Lutheran theological interpretations of Scripture often overlap with devotional readings of Scripture. Both are intended to answer the "So what?" question: What does this Bible text mean to me/us here and now in our contemporary situation?

The first exercise asks participants to compare 1 Corinthians 12:1-11 with Luther's explanation of the Third Article of the Apostles' Creed from the Small Catechism. Participants will come to see how deeply Luther's theology is informed by Scripture, even when he does not quote or refer to any particular biblical text. Here both Scripture and Lutheran theology emphasize that the Holy Spirit should get all the credit for our belief in, commitment to, and faith in Jesus Christ.

The second activity involves a quick survey of a number of Bible texts linked by the common theme that those who lack status, power, and honor should be treated with dignity and respect. Ancient scriptures and traditions highlight this theme, Jesus exemplified it in his life and ministry, and Paul continues on with it. Aliens are to be loved as citizens (Leviticus 19:33-34), God welcomes eunuchs and aliens (Isaiah 56:1-8), the disciples are not to lord it over their followers (Matthew 20:24-28), and Jesus sets an example for the disciples by washing their feet (John 13:1-17).

Whether participants hear the Bible text as gospel or law will depend on their own personal circumstances and experiences.

DEVOTIONAL CONTEXT

The Focus Statement for this session is "The Holy Spirit gives each person a gift that is indispensable to the body of Christ." Discerning that gift enables a person to answer the question, "What am I good for?" Yet we are not always the best judges of our own gifts and contributions to the body of Christ. We tend to either over- or underestimate our gifts, so in this section participants are asked to identify gifts or blessings that others bring to the group. Ensure that each person is honored for at least one spiritual gift or blessing, and point out the variety of gifts present among the group.

In the orders for Baptism and Affirmation of Baptism in ELW, we pray that God will sustain us and stir up in us the gift of the Holy Spirit. This is an excellent reminder that the Holy Spirit has been

SESSION FOUR

with us for a long time. Encourage participants to reflect on how the Holy Spirit has been active in their lives up to this point, and on what new gifts, ministries, or activities the Holy Spirit may be leading them into now.

Facilitator's Prayer

Lord Jesus Christ, in the church that is your body here on earth there is room for every person. Thank you for making room for me. Thank you for your gifts of the Spirit, of faith and courage to lead others in studying your Word. Enable me to see the gifts of all members of this study group, to affirm their contributions, and to treat them with dignity and respect. Be with me, Jesus, I pray. Amen.

Gather (10-15 minutes)

Check-in

Invite learners to share completed homework or any new thoughts or insights about the last session. Be ready to give a brief recap of that session if necessary.

Pray

Almighty God, your Holy Spirit equips the church with a rich variety of gifts. Grant that we may use them to bear witness to Christ in lives that are built on faith and love. Make us ready to live the gospel and eager to do your will, so that we may share with all your church in the joys of eternal life; through Jesus Christ, our Savior and Lord. Amen. (ELW, p. 76)

Focus Activity

Take a few moments to examine the Focus Image. How does a finger, hand, eye, or toe contribute to the overall functioning and well-being of a human body? Reflecting on your membership in the church, what part of the body do you feel most like, and why?

Tip:
If group members wish, they may add or substitute extemporaneous prayers and petitions reflecting the highs and lows of their weeks. This may be done as a "circle" prayer in which each person gives thanks or asks for one thing in prayer.

Tip:
Group members may be more comfortable doing this activity as a silent meditation with opportunity for journaling. Make sure everyone has paper and pencils or pens.

Open Scripture (10-15 minutes)

Have participants form two groups. Assign 1 Corinthians 12:1-11, 27-31 to one group and 1 Corinthians 12:12-26 to the other. Invite

SESSION FOUR

each group to retell Paul's message collaboratively and creatively through art, music, drama, or sign language.

Have someone read 1 Corinthians 12:1-11. Give hearers a few minutes to jot down words or phrases that captured their attention, or images that were evoked by the text. Repeat with 1 Corinthians 12:12-31. Ask participants to share their thoughts.

Read 1 Corinthians 12:1-31.
- What words or phrases caught your attention?
- What people or situations were called to mind?
- What issues or concerns does this text raise for you?

Join the Conversation (25-55 minutes)

Historical Context

1. The topic in 1 Corinthians 12:1-11 is *pneumatika*, literally phenomena induced by the Spirit, but usually translated as "spiritual gifts." In the cultural environment of ancient Mediterranean societies, the existence of spirits, both good and bad, was taken for granted. The challenge was to discern what phenomena were genuinely induced by God's Holy Spirit.
- Look over 1 Corinthians 12:1-11. What criteria does Paul suggest for discerning who or what is truly inspired by the Spirit?

2. Greco-Roman political rhetoric frequently presented the body as a symbol of society in order to encourage social harmony. This political rhetoric insisted that a healthy body (society) was one in which every part was in its proper place and doing its assigned tasks. The head and its parts (mind, eyes, ears, and so on) had the highest status, providing direction and guidance for the rest of the body. The lowest-ranking parts (persons) were covered up, hidden from public view, and without public voice. The end goal of this rhetoric was to reinforce and maintain the distinctions that separated rulers from those they ruled over.
- Read 1 Corinthians 12:12-31 and compare Paul's idea of the church as the body of Christ to the Greco-Roman political rhetoric about society as a body. What aspects of the body does Paul emphasize?
- Imagine how the different members of Paul's congregation in Corinth would hear and respond to this teaching. Who was Paul

Tip:
It might be helpful to review the discussion of daimons from Session 3 to provide background for the conversation on Spirit-induced phenomena.

Bonus Activity:
In our culture few people talk about Spirit-induced behaviors or states. There is, however, interest in altered states of consciousness. Do an online search on "altered states of consciousness" to see the number and variety of articles on this topic.

Bonus Activity:
We use the body and body parts in our contemporary culture as metaphors that are often value-laden. For example, consider the meaning of calling someone "high-minded" versus saying someone else is "ruled by his belly." Have participants brainstorm and reflect on ways that we use "body language" today.

SESSION FOUR

trying to affirm and empower? Who was Paul trying to correct and change? Discuss whether this type of affirmation and correction is needed in the church today.

Literary Context

1. Paul says in the session Scripture text that through the Holy Spirit God activates or energizes three forms of *pneumatika*: *charismata*—gifts or graces given to the individual, *diakonia*—service-oriented ministries, and *energemata*—energizing or inspiring activities.

- List the spiritual gifts mentioned by Paul in 1 Corinthians 12:8-10 and 12:28. Which of these gifts would you identify as individual gifts or graces? Service-oriented ministries? Energizing or inspiring activities?
- Are all of the spiritual gifts that Paul mentions still active in the church today? Are some gifts more prevalent than others?

2. Some members of the church in Corinth were arguing that speaking in tongues was more important than other spiritual gifts. Paul's response to this argument is in 1 Corinthians 13 and 14.

- Read 1 Corinthians 13 and list the characteristics of love and of speaking in tongues and other spiritual gifts. What similarities and differences do you see? How does this connect with Paul's comments in 1 Corinthians 12:7 and 12:21-26?
- How might Paul's vision of love shape the way we think about being the body of Christ?

Lutheran Context

1. Martin Luther explains the work of the Holy Spirit in individuals, the church, and the world in his explanation of the Third Article of the Apostles' Creed ("I believe in the Holy Spirit . . ."):

> I believe that by my own understanding or strength I cannot believe in Jesus Christ my Lord or come to him, but instead the Holy Spirit has called me through the gospel, enlightened me with his gifts, made me holy, and kept me in the true faith, just as he calls, gathers, enlightens, and makes holy the whole Christian church on earth and keeps it with Jesus Christ in the one common, true faith. (*Luther's Small Catechism with* Evangelical Lutheran Worship *Texts* [Augsburg Fortress, 2008], 16)

Tip:
It may be beneficial to have participants working in small groups on these activities. Make sure there is time for each working group to share insights with the large group.

Bonus Activity:
Paul takes up the question of spiritual gifts again in Romans 12:4-8, and his teaching also informs Ephesians 4:7-13. Compare these two texts with Paul's comments in 1 Corinthians 12:8-10 and 12:28. What is the consistent message about spiritual gifts in these texts?

Bonus Activity:
Paul describes the relative merits of two spiritual gifts, prophecy and speaking in tongues (*glossolalia*), in 1 Corinthians 14:1-25. We often think of prophecy as predicting the future, but Paul is talking about inspired preaching that admonishes, consoles, builds up, and encourages believers. Speaking in tongues, as Paul describes it, is speech that is "not intelligible" to anyone without interpretation. Read 1 Corinthians 14:1-25 and identify what Paul is trying to tell his readers in Corinth.

Tip:
You will need copies of *Evangelical Lutheran Worship* for the Bonus Activity and for the Devotional Context.

Session 4: 1 Corinthians 12:1-31   41

SESSION FOUR

 Bonus Activity:
Look at the words to the hymn "Spirit of God, Descend upon My Heart" (ELW 800). This hymn is really a prayer. What is the singer asking for? How does this hymn express the Lutheran theological convictions discussed in this session?

- What words and phrases in this statement help us better understand what Paul is trying to get at in 1 Corinthians 12:1-11? How does Paul's message help us understand Luther's point in the Small Catechism?

2. Using the Lutheran principle of "Scripture interprets Scripture," we read passages from other parts of the Bible to shed light on the meaning of a text.

- Read Leviticus 19:33-34; Isaiah 56:1-8; Matthew 20:24-28; and John 13:1-17. What is the main point or lesson in each of these texts? How do these texts help us understand Paul's teaching in 1 Corinthians 12:12-26? How does Paul's message help us understand these other passages?

3. Lutherans read Scripture through the lenses of law and gospel. Law judges and convicts us and challenges us to change our ways. Gospel causes God's grace and love to reach out to us, comforting and sustaining us. Law and gospel are present throughout the Bible.

- When you read 1 Corinthians 12:12-26, where do you hear law? Where do you hear gospel?

Devotional Context

1. The Focus Statement for this session is "The Holy Spirit gives each person a gift that is indispensable to the body of Christ." Go around the room and name a gift or blessing that each person contributes to the group. You might use the following format:

[*Name*], you are good for [*gift or blessing*].

 Tip:
If your group is particularly large, it might be more efficient to have each participant name one gift that the person beside him or her brings. Another option is to give participants brightly colored sticky notes on which to write a gift or blessing they have experienced in the group. Arrange these on a poster board titled "Gifts of the Spirit in Our Group."

2. The Holy Spirit is given to us in the sacrament of Holy Baptism. Reflect on how the Holy Spirit has been and is still active in your life. Share your thoughts with the group.

Wrap-up

1. If there are any questions to explore further, write them on chart paper or a whiteboard. Ask for volunteers to do further research to share with the group at the next session.

 Bonus Activity:
Invite the group to brainstorm a list of spiritual gifts that are present within your congregation.

2. As time allows, invite participants to reflect on what they have learned in this session. What new perspectives have they gained?

Pray

We give you thanks, O God, that through water and the Holy Spirit you give us new birth, cleanse us from sin, and raise us to eternal life.

SESSION FOUR

Stir up in your people the gift of your Holy Spirit: the spirit of wisdom and understanding, the spirit of counsel and might, the spirit of knowledge and the fear of the Lord, the spirit of joy in your presence, both now and forever. Amen. (ELW, p. 237)

Extending the Conversation (5 minutes)

Homework

1. Read the next session's Bible text: 1 Corinthians 15:12-28, 35-58.

2. To discover your own spiritual gifts, complete the spiritual gifts assessment available at www.elca.org/Growing-in-Faith/Ministry/Women-of-the-ELCA/All-Our-Resources/Affirming-Our-Gifts/Spiritual-Gifts-Discovery.aspx. Once you have completed the assessment, reflect on how you use your gifts to build up the body of Christ. Perhaps it's time to become more involved in some way!

3. Look around your congregation and/or community. Who feels weak, dispensable, less honorable, or less respectable? Why do they feel that way? Are there things you could do to change that? What can you do to show these people that they are honored and respected and appreciated for their presence? Make a plan and act on it. Get others involved too.

Enrichment

1. If you want to read all of 1 and 2 Corinthians during this unit, read the following sections this week.
- Day 1: 1 Corinthians 13:1-13
- Day 2: 1 Corinthians 14:1-25
- Day 3: 1 Corinthians 14:26-40
- Day 4: 1 Corinthians 15:1-11
- Day 5: 1 Corinthians 15:12-34
- Day 6: 1 Corinthians 15:35-58
- Day 7: 1 Corinthians 16:1-24

2. Read the ABC News *Nightline* story "Speaking in Tongues: Alternative Voices in Faith" at http://abcnews.go.com/Nightline/story?id=2935819&page=1. Reflect on your reactions and thoughts about speaking in tongues.

Tip:
You may wish to gather around the baptismal font for the closing prayer. Participants may dip their fingers in the water and make the sign of the cross on their foreheads in thanksgiving for the gift of the Spirit received in baptism.

Tip:
Encourage learners to do the spiritual gifts assessment and to use this as a basis for becoming involved in a new ministry in the congregation.

SESSION FOUR

For Further Reading

Yung Suk Kim, *Christ's Body in Corinth: The Politics of a Metaphor* (Fortress Press, 2008).

Lois Malcolm, *Holy Spirit: Creative Power in Our Lives* (Augsburg Fortress, 2009).

Dale B. Martin, *The Corinthian Body* (Yale University Press, 1999).

Looking Ahead

1. Read the next session's Bible text: 1 Corinthians 15:12-28, 35-58.

2. Read through the Leader Guide for the next session and mark portions you wish to highlight for the group.

3. Make a checklist of any materials you'll need to do the Bonus Activities.

4. Pray for members of your group during the week.

SESSION FIVE

1 Corinthians
15:12-28, 35-58

Leader
Session
Guide

Focus Statement

In the resurrection we will be like Christ and with Christ in God, who will be all in all.

Key Verse

Just as we have borne the image of the man of dust, we will also bear the image of the man of heaven.
1 Corinthians 15:49

Focus Image

© Nadya Lukio / iStockphoto

Eschatology:

Literally means the study or knowledge of the "last things," specifically the final or ultimate destiny of individual persons, humanity as a whole, and all of creation. Personal eschatology deals with the destiny of individuals, while cosmic eschatology deals with the destiny of creation, including humanity as a whole.

What Will I Be Ultimately?

Session Preparation

Before You Begin . . .

The session title is a play on that familiar question, "What do you want to be when you grow up?" When you were a child, how did you answer that question? What did you want to be? When you look ahead, what do you want to be at the end of your earthly journey? What do you want to be ultimately, after your earthly journey, in eternity?

Session Instructions

1. Read this Session Guide completely and highlight or underline any portions you wish to emphasize with the group. Note any Bonus Activities you wish to do.

2. If you plan to do any special activities, check to see what materials you'll need, if any.

3. Have extra Bibles on hand in case a member of the group forgets to bring one.

Session Overview

The session Scripture text from 1 Corinthians 15 deals with **eschatology,** the study of last things, specifically the final or ultimate destiny of individuals, humanity as a whole, and all of creation. In this session participants learn that our personal destinies are embedded in and utterly dependent on Christ's **resurrection,** which inaugurates Christ's rule in the world. As we await Christ's return, we are called to be steadfast in doing the Lord's work.

Historical Context

We begin by looking at Paul's eschatological message within the context of first-century Corinth, where people had differing opinions about the afterlife. Some believed there was no afterlife. Others thought that the souls of the dead lived on in Hades, which was divided into nasty and nice regions. Still others said the souls of those initiated into the mystery religions would ascend to the heavens. Greco-Roman eschatology involving the survival of the soul was rooted in beliefs about the inferiority of the physical body, which was seen as a prison or tomb for the soul.

SESSION FIVE

 Resurrection:
Literally means "to stand up again." It is the ancient biblical conviction that there will be real embodied life in the new world or age to come that God will establish.

In light of these beliefs, the idea of a bodily resurrection into a new world and age established by God would have been strange, even repugnant. Yet that is precisely what Paul argues for.

A careful reading of 1 Corinthians 15:12-28, 35-58 demonstrates that Paul consistently embeds personal eschatology within cosmic eschatology. In other words, the ultimate destiny of individual believers depends upon the historical event of Christ's resurrection, which inaugurates the new age—the kingdom of God in this world. Believers will be resurrected into a transformed life in this kingdom when Christ returns to overcome all the forces that oppose God, including death. The end goal of this cosmic renewal is that God will be all in all (1 Corinthians 15:28). Individual believers will bear the image of Christ in eternity (15:49). Thus, in keeping with his Jewish roots, Paul promotes a vision of a life beyond the grave and an afterlife that involves not just individual souls but all of creation.

Literary Context

In 1 Corinthians 15:12-28 Paul highlights four events in Christian cosmic eschatology:

- Christ's resurrection inaugurating his kingship/kingdom;
- Christ's return, which triggers the resurrection of believers;
- Christ's overcoming of all forces opposed to God, concluding with death; and
- Christ's handing over the kingdom so that God may be all in all.

This text is only one of several Scriptures dealing with our ultimate destiny. Various Christian groups tend to highlight different eschatological teachings:

- the transformation of all creation (Romans 8:18-24);
- the presence of good and evil until the final judgment (Matthew 13:24-30);
- the "rapture" (1 Thessalonians 4:13-18); or
- the millennial kingdom of Christ (Revelation 20:1-15).

Soma psychikon:
This term, usually mistranslated as "physical body," literally means a "soul-body" or a "mind-body." To use a computer analogy, it refers to a body in which the operating system is a rational soul or mind.

In 1 Corinthians 15:35-58 Paul describes the transformation of believers' bodies when Christ returns. "Pre-resurrection bodies" (***soma psychikon***) are perishable, associated with dishonor and weakness, physical, like the first Adam (living being), from the earth or of dust, flesh and blood, and mortal. "Post-resurrection bodies" (**soma pneumatikon**) are imperishable, associated with glory (radiance) and power, spiritual, like the last Adam (life-giving spirit), from heaven, not flesh and blood, and immortal.

Though *psychikon* is often translated as "physical," participants are asked to note the problems associated with this translation. The goal here is to emphasize that for Paul resurrection is not about separating the immortal soul from its bodily prison but about transformation of the whole person—body, mind, and soul—into a new mode of being.

 Soma pneumatikon: This term is usually translated as "spiritual body." It does not mean a body without substance. To return to the computer analogy, it means a body in which the operating system is spirit, perhaps even the Holy Spirit.

Lutheran Context

The Nicene and Apostles' Creeds were developed by the early church as summaries of the central beliefs of Christianity. The Lutheran church has historically accepted them as true statements of our faith. Participants will read these creeds carefully, looking for eschatological elements—statements pointing to the ultimate destiny of believers, humanity, and the world.

Cosmic eschatology lies behind the following affirmations:
- God is creator of all life.
- Christ will return to judge the living and the dead.
- Christ's kingdom will have no end (Nicene Creed).
- the resurrection of the dead
- the life of the world to come (Nicene Creed)

Personal eschatology is indicated by references to baptism and the forgiveness of sins; but there is no sustained conversation about the final fate of individual persons or souls.

These creeds thus stand in continuity with the biblical emphasis on cosmic eschatology.

The Lutheran reformers, like Paul, rejected ancient Greek views of the soul as an immortal or divine element imprisoned in a material human body and longing for escape from physical existence. Instead, in continuity with biblical thought, the reformers regarded the human person more holistically. Body, mind, and soul are equally affected by sin and are equally in need of healing and redemption. Comparing and contrasting Paul's descriptions of pre- and post-resurrection bodies can provide insights into the effects of sin and the nature of the healing that God seeks to accomplish in us personally.

SESSION FIVE

DEVOTIONAL CONTEXT

The Focus Image is offered as an attempt to represent Paul's idea of a transformed humanity in a creation freed from bondage to sin and death. Participants will be asked to contemplate this image and consider what it suggests about life in the resurrection. How does this image answer the question, "What will I be ultimately?"

Participants will then be asked to look again at the pictures and symbols they drew at the beginning of the session to depict their own ideas about their final destiny. What are the similarities and differences between their pictures and the Focus Image? Would participants change anything in their drawings after having studied 1 Corinthians 15?

In the final devotional activity, participants are asked to think about the significance of the session Scripture texts in their daily lives, their vocations, and the congregation's mission. Is this only speculation about a future that remains beyond our grasp? Does it have anything to teach us in the present? Does knowing that Scripture promises that our final destiny is to bear the image of Christ affect the way we live our lives on a daily basis? Does knowing that the end goal of history is that "God will be all in all" (1 Corinthians 15:28) affect how we view the world? Does it help clarify what our mission and purpose are or ought to be here and now? Paul suggests an answer in 1 Corinthians 15:58.

Facilitator's Prayer

Gracious God, there are no words to adequately express my gratitude for the life, death, and resurrection of your beloved Son, Jesus Christ. Because he lives, I too will live always in your presence. Be with our group as we gather to hear this good news. Open our ears to hear your Word, our eyes to see you ever-present in the world around us, and our hearts to your gifts of faith, hope, and love. In Jesus' name I pray. Amen.

Gather (10-15 minutes)

Check-in

Invite learners to share completed homework or any new thoughts or insights about the last session. Be ready to give a brief recap of that session if necessary.

SESSION FIVE

Pray

God of mercy, we no longer look for Jesus among the dead, for he is alive and has become the Lord of life. Increase in our minds and hearts the risen life we share with Christ, and help us to grow as your people toward the fullness of eternal life with you, through Jesus Christ, our Savior and Lord, who lives and reigns with you and the Holy Spirit, one God, now and forever. Amen. (ELW, p. 32)

Focus Activity

How would you answer the question, "What will I be ultimately?" Draw, sketch, or doodle a picture, image, or symbol representing your understanding of your final destiny.

 Tip:
If group members prefer, they may add or substitute extemporaneous prayers and petitions reflecting the highs and lows of their week. This may be done as a "circle prayer" in which each person gives thanks or asks for one thing in prayer.

 Tip:
Provide participants with paper, colored pencils, markers, or crayons for this activity. Invite participants to share their thoughts or sketches with the group as they are comfortable doing so.

Open Scripture (10-15 minutes)

Invite participants to jot down words and phrases, doodle, or sketch images that come to mind as you or someone else reads 1 Corinthians 15:12-28 slowly and with care for its meaning. Stop and take a moment to reflect and share. Repeat with 1 Corinthians 15:35-58.

Ask volunteers to read in turn 15:12-19; 15:20-28; 15:35-41; 15:42-49; 15:50-58. At the end of each segment, pause for a moment of reflection and ask participants to jot down the most important idea they heard.

Read 1 Corinthians 15:12-28, 35-58.
- What words or phrases caught your attention?
- What images, sounds, or situations do these texts call to mind?
- What questions do these passages raise for you?

Join the Conversation (25-55 minutes)

Historical Context

1. Ancient peoples had differing opinions about the "end" or final destiny of individual persons, entire societies, and the world itself. Greco-Roman beliefs focused on individuals—what happens to people when they die. While some Greeks and Romans insisted that this life is all there is, most believed the souls of the dead went to nasty or nice regions of Hades,

 Tip:
The ancient Greek idea of the body as a tomb was introduced in Session 3. You might want to review that material with participants.

SESSION FIVE

 Bonus Activity:
Have participants view Professor James Tabor's collection of Greek and Roman writings and tomb inscriptions on the Web page "The Jewish Roman World of Jesus" at http://www.religiousstudies.uncc.edu/JDTABOR/dualism.html.

 Bonus Activity:
To get a sense of the range of ancient Israelite beliefs about this issue, have participants look up the following passages: Psalm 88:3-12; 1 Samuel 28:3-25; Job 14:10-12; Ecclesiastes 3:19-20; Isaiah 11:6-9; Daniel 12:1-2.

 Tip:
It might be time-wise to have participants form two working groups, one to concentrate on the questions associated with 1 Corinthians 15:20-28, the other to do those associated with 15:35-58. Have group members post their answers on a whiteboard or chart paper to share with the whole group. Ensure that there is time for whole group discussion.

 Bonus Activity:
The Gospels record Jesus' teachings about the resurrection of the dead. Look up Matthew 22:23-33; Matthew 25:31-46; John 5:25-29; and John 11:17-27. Although originating as descriptions of first-century historical events, texts like Mark 13:14-27 have also been interpreted as dealing with the end. How do these texts expand your understanding of the resurrection and/or Christ's second coming?

depending on what they deserved. Many people were initiated into various mystery religions, hoping that at death their souls would be freed from imprisonment in physical bodies and join the gods in the starry heavens.

- Compare Greco-Roman beliefs about the end with the session Scripture text. What similarities and differences do you see?

2. Israelites imagined the souls of the dead residing in an underworld called Sheol. By the first century, many believed the souls of the righteous were gathered into a heavenly place (such as Abraham's bosom). Some within Judaism insisted that our final destiny lay beyond the afterlife: resurrection of the body into a new life in a new world and a new age established by God. The focus of Israelite beliefs about the end, however, was not only on what happens to individuals when they die, but on God's ultimate plan for all of creation—what happens to the heavens and the earth and all they contain.

- What is Paul trying to explain in 1 Corinthians 15:12-28 and 15:35-58? How does this text compare with Jewish beliefs about the end? What does Paul focus on?

Literary Context

1. Major themes in Christian beliefs about the end are derived from the session Scripture text and other New Testament passages. In 1 Corinthians 15, Paul writes about the ultimate goal of Christ's mission, and key events in the unfolding of that mission.

- Read 1 Corinthians 15:20-28 closely. Identify what Paul understands to be the ultimate goal of Christ's mission in human history, and four key events that take place as that mission unfolds. Are these past, present, or future events?
- Identify what the following texts say about the end, and discuss whether all of these are equally important for understanding the goals and purposes of Christ's mission as we participate in it here and now.

> Romans 8:18-24
> 1 Thessalonians 4:13-18
> Matthew 13:24-30
> Revelation 20:1-15

2. To drive home what he is saying, Paul contrasts "pre-resurrection bodies" with "post-resurrection bodies." List the characteristics of each type of body, as described in 1 Corinthians 15:35-58. How are these bodies similar? How are they different?

SESSION FIVE

3. It is often difficult to translate terms precisely from one language to another. Consider this: In 1 Corinthians 15:44 Paul distinguishes between two different kinds of bodies using the Greek phrases *soma psychikon* versus *soma pneumatikon*. While *pneumatikon* does mean "spiritual," *psychikon* derives from the Greek word *psyche*, often translated as "soul" or "life principle." Greek-speaking Jews like Paul often used *psyche* to refer to "mind." It is the root of our English term *psychology*, the study of mental functions and behaviors.

- Discuss what it might mean that in the resurrection *psyche* will be transformed into *pneuma*. What is the distinction that Paul is trying to draw? How does this compare with what you believe about the end?

Lutheran Context

1. The Lutheran reformers accepted the Nicene Creed and the Apostles' Creed as true statements of the Christian faith. Lutherans today continue to accept these creeds and use them in worship.

- Read the words of the Nicene Creed and the Apostles' Creed (ELW, pp. 104–105). What is the primary focus of these creeds—the ultimate destiny of individual persons or of all creation? What words and phrases support your conclusions?

2. In the Formula of Concord the Lutheran reformers write, "concerning the article on the resurrection Scripture testifies that this very substance of our flesh, albeit without sin, will rise, and that we will have and retain this soul, albeit without sin, in eternal life" (*The Book of Concord: The Confessions of the Evangelical Lutheran Church*, ed. Robert Kolb and Timothy J. Wengert [Fortress Press, 2000], 539.46). What they are saying is that the whole person (body, mind, soul) will be resurrected into eternal life, but without sin and its effects.

- How does this Lutheran theological insight help us to see what the difference is between pre-resurrection and post-resurrection bodies (1 Corinthians 15:35-58)? How does Paul's description of post-resurrection bodies help us better understand how sin affects human beings?

Devotional Context

1. Spend a few moments just looking at the Focus Image, then discuss the following questions:

Bonus Activity:
Jesus' teaching as recorded in the Gospels includes references to individual resurrection or life after death. Look up Matthew 10:28-33; Luke 16:19-31; and Luke 23:39-43. Are these biblical texts consistent with others?

Tip:
The historical creeds and Lutheran confessions are intended to provide Lutheran Christians with guides to navigate and identify what is truly central to the faith in the often confusing world of biblical interpretation.

Bonus Activity:
The Lutheran confessional position on end times is called *amillenialism*, a position we share with most mainline denominations. Give participants a quick introduction to this teaching by having them read the article "Amillenialism" at http://en.wikipedia.org/wiki/Amillenialism.

Bonus Activity:
Take a look at a segment of a videotaped interview with Barbara Rossing, professor at Lutheran Theological Seminary at Chicago and author of *The Rapture Exposed*, on the dangers of the "so-called rapture" at http://www.youtube.com/watch?v=frqIH5eATWg (3:36 minutes in length).

SESSION FIVE

Tip:
If there is time, have participants share their responses to the questions listed under #2 in pairs.

Bonus Activity:
Read Romans 6:1-14. Here Paul writes that in baptism we are united with Christ, both in his death and in his resurrection. How is that good news to you? What evidence is there in your life that you are dying to sin and alive to God?

- As an illustration of life in the resurrection, what does this photograph suggest about what it means to be like Christ? What does it imply about being with Christ in God? What does it say about where God is and will be?
- How does this image compare with the one you drew at the beginning of this session? Looking back on that picture now, would you change anything? Why or why not?

2. Write down your responses to these questions:
- How is the session Scripture text good news for you personally? How does the promise that you will one day bear the image of "the man of heaven" (1 Corinthians 15:49) affect the way you live your life on a daily basis?
- What difference does Christ's resurrection make in how you view the world in which you live? How does Paul's statement that the end goal of Christ's mission is that God will be all in all (1 Corinthians 15:28) affect your personal vocation and/or the mission of your congregation?

Wrap-up

1. If there are any questions to explore further, write them on chart paper or a whiteboard. Ask for volunteers to do further research to share with the group at the next session.

2. As time allows, invite participants to reflect on what they have learned in this session. What new perspectives have they gained?

Pray

Lord of Life, whom death could not hold, we praise and adore you. Your resurrection was unexpected, amazing, and almost unbelievable, but now we know that the grave is not our final destiny. Now we can be sure that nothing is hopeless. Broken relationships . . . sickness . . . distress of any kind . . . conflict . . . and even death . . . will not have the final word. Because you live we can live life to the fullest, knowing that we have everything to live for today, tomorrow, and forever. Amen.

Tip:
During the prayer, pause after each of the items in the sentence that begins with "Broken relationships . . . sickness . . ." and so on. Invite group members to add their own concerns aloud or silently if they wish.

SESSION FIVE

Extending the Conversation (5 minutes)

Homework

1. Read the next session's Bible text: 2 Corinthians 3:1—4:15.

2. Spend some time each day reflecting on what you have learned in this session. How is each day of your life a step toward that final destiny? This might be an opportunity for some soul-searching. Is God "all" in your life? What stands in the way of God becoming "all"? If God were "all," how would your daily life be different?

3. Begin each day by reading 1 Corinthians 15:58. Make it the goal of your day to be steadfast in doing the Lord's work in all the situations and places where you find yourself. Take time to identify situations and places—big and small—where you see God at work or where the gospel is needed, and consider how you might be part of that work.

Enrichment

1. If you want to read all of 1 and 2 Corinthians during this unit, read the following sections this week.
- Day 1: 1 Corinthians 15:35-58
- Day 2: 1 Corinthians 16:1-24
- Day 3: 2 Corinthians 1:1-11
- Day 4: 2 Corinthians 1:12—2:4
- Day 5: 2 Corinthians 2:5-17
- Day 6: 2 Corinthians 3:1-18
- Day 7: 2 Corinthians 4:1-15

2. Part 3 of Handel's sacred oratorio *Messiah* is based on selected verses from 1 Corinthians 15. Listen to a recording or performance of this music. How does Handel's musical interpretation affect your understanding of Paul's message?

3. Make time to view the film *What Dreams May Come* (1998), starring Robin Williams and Cuba Gooding Jr. How are the beliefs about final destiny depicted in the film similar to and/or different from biblical understandings of what Christ does for us?

Tip:
Encourage learners to continue journaling about their thoughts and reflections on each session and the Homework and Enrichment activities.

SESSION FIVE

For Further Reading

Alister E. McGrath, *Resurrection* (Fortress Press, 2007).

Barbara R. Rossing, *The Rapture Exposed: The Message of Hope in the Book of Revelation* (Basic Books, 2004).

Robert B. Stewart, ed., *The Resurrection of Jesus: John Dominic Crossan and N. T. Wright in Dialogue* (Fortress Press, 2005).

Looking Ahead

1. Read the next session's Bible text: 2 Corinthians 3:1—4:15.

2. Read through the Leader Guide for the next session and mark portions you wish to highlight for the group.

3. Make a checklist of any materials you'll need to do the Bonus Activities.

4. Pray for members of your group during the week.

SESSION SIX

2 Corinthians 3:1—4:15

Leader Session Guide

Focus Statement
Our transformation into the image of Christ is entirely the work of the Holy Spirit.

Key Verse
And all of us, with unveiled faces, seeing the glory of the Lord as though reflected in a mirror, are being transformed into the same image from one degree of glory to another; for this comes from the Lord, the Spirit. 2 Corinthians 3:18

Focus Image

FreeWine (Flickr). Used by Creative Commons 2.0 Attribution License.

Gentiles:
Non-Jews; in other words, everyone who is not Jewish. In Paul's day, 95 to 97 percent of the population of the Roman Empire was not Jewish and believed in many gods. Today "Gentiles" include Christians and Muslims.

How Do I Achieve This Glory?

Session Preparation

Before You Begin . . .

In our last session we learned that our final destiny is to be like Christ and with Christ. Now we turn to the question, "How do I achieve this glory?" What do you think it will take for you to be like Christ? What has to happen to make that a reality? What will you have to give up? What will you have to do that you don't do now? Can you accomplish this by your own will and power?

Session Instructions

1. Read this Session Guide completely and highlight or underline any portions you wish to emphasize with the group. Note any Bonus Activities you wish to do.

2. If you plan to do any special activities, check to see what materials you'll need, if any.

3. Have extra Bibles on hand in case a member of the group forgets to bring one.

Session Overview

Second Corinthians 3:1—4:15 is Paul's response to rivals claiming that, in order to be saved, believers must do the things prescribed by the letter of the old covenant. Paul rejects such claims in strong language. He is adamant that in the new covenant, believers are saved as the Holy Spirit transforms them gradually into the image of Jesus Christ. We cannot achieve this glory on our own. It is the work of the Holy Spirit.

HISTORICAL CONTEXT

Jesus, his disciples, and all the earliest members of the churches grew up in the Jewish faith. As **Gentiles** joined fledgling congregations in Judea and Syria, a question arose over how people are saved. Not surprisingly, some leaders insisted that Gentiles had to become Torah-observant Jews if they wished to be part of these early Christian congregations. Others, like Paul, argued that the Holy Spirit's presence and gifts in the lives of Gentile converts proved that God had accepted them; so there was no need for them to become Jews. Acts 10–15 portrays the apostles reaching a compromise agreement on this question at the Jerusalem Council (49 C.E.). Paul's version of that event in Galatians 2 suggests something slightly different. In fact, all of the letters he wrote in the following decade provide evidence of an

SESSION SIX

ongoing and heated debate in the churches. Paul's understanding of salvation was thus forged in the real world of religious experience and conflict. He was no armchair theologian.

The activities in the Historical Context will introduce participants to these background issues. They will see that Paul describes the old covenant in strongly negative terms. However, his language should not be read as anti-Jewish or anti-Semitic. Remind participants that Paul and his opponents were all Jews equally committed to living out the message of the Hebrew Scriptures in light of Christ. This historical background should enable learners to summarize Paul's message about salvation in their own words and draw connections to contemporary issues.

LITERARY CONTEXT

Paul reinterprets the main elements of Exodus 34 in light of the Corinthians' experiences in Christ. He operates with a logic of "If x is good, how much better is y."

> **Jewish Christians:**
> The apostles, disciples, and earliest followers of Christ, including Paul, were all ethnically and religiously Jewish.

Old covenant	New covenant
Stone tablets (2 Corinthians 3:3, 7; Exodus 34:1, 4)	Tablets of human hearts (2 Corinthians 3:3)
Old covenant of letters (2 Corinthians 3:14; Exodus 34:10-28)	New covenant of Spirit (2 Corinthians 3:6)
Encountering God results in Moses' shining face (2 Corinthians 3:7; Exodus 34:29-30)	The Spirit transforms believers into the image of Christ (2 Corinthians 3:8-11, 18)
The veil over Moses' face (2 Corinthians 3:13; Exodus 34:33)	The veil over the minds of **Jewish Christian** peers (2 Corinthians 3:14-15)
Moses takes off the veil before the Lord (2 Corinthians 3:16; Exodus 34:34)	Christ removes the veil from those who turn to him (2 Corinthians 3:14, 16)

Paul does not read Exodus literally. His interpretation presupposes the ancient convictions that

- Scripture is cryptic and mysterious, always meaning more than it says; hence to read it literally is to miss out on that additional meaning.
- Scripture is eternally valid, so people and events in the text stand for themselves as well as contemporary persons and events (see 2 Corinthians 3:14-16).

Paul reads Exodus 34 theologically to claim that salvation is not the result of doing the things prescribed in the Law of Moses. Rather, salvation is entirely the Holy Spirit's work. To demonstrate this, Paul uses images in 2 Corinthians 4:6-15 that contrast human fragility with the gospel's power. It is God who enlightens and empowers us to overcome life's afflictions and, in doing so, conforms us to the death and resurrected life of Jesus.

Lutheran Context

In the first-century church, some leaders insisted that humans could achieve eternal glory by carrying out the Law of Moses. We hear similar messages today, demanding that we do something, make some decision, read the Bible in a certain way, live a certain lifestyle, or engage in some religious practice in order to be saved.

Martin Luther's explanation of the Third Article of the Apostles' Creed could serve as a paraphrase of Paul's message in the session Scripture text. Reading 2 Corinthians 3:1—4:15 through this lens helps us answer the question, "How do I achieve this glory?" Luther reminds us that salvation is a gift from God, not something we achieve.

A simplistic reading of 2 Corinthians 3:1-18 might conclude that the old covenant is of no value to members of the new. Lutheran theology rejects such an interpretation. Luther insists that letter and spirit do not refer to two covenants or even the two testaments in the Bible, but to two kinds of preaching that are found throughout both the Old and New Testament. **Law** and **gospel** relate not so much to the content of Scripture as to its effects on us. When we hear demands, expectations, and judgments against us, we experience Scripture as law. The Holy Spirit uses this experience to open us up to the transformative power of the gospel experienced as comfort, grace, and healing. This means that each of us experiences law and gospel differently and according to where we are in our journey of faith.

Devotional Context

The contemplation and discussion of "How do I achieve this glory?" comes full circle here. The "glory" referred to is the glory of the resurrected Christ, whose image we are to bear. In 2 Corinthians 3:18, Paul writes that all of us see this glory now, but only as reflected in a mirror. Thinking back on the Focus Activity, participants will consider where they see God reflected in the world in the lives and actions of others around them, and how others might see God reflected in them.

The Devotional Context encourages participants to respond on a more personal level to Paul's teaching and the question, "How do I achieve this glory?" Perhaps this session has simply affirmed their

> **? Law:**
> In Lutheran theology, the law is a word of God that we experience as a demand, expectation, or judgment, regardless of whether it is in the Old or New Testament and what type of writing (commandment, parable, etc.) it is.

> **? Gospel:**
> In Lutheran theology, the gospel is a word of God that we experience as grace, comfort, or healing, regardless of whether it is in the Old or New Testament and what type of writing (commandment, parable, etc.) it is.

SESSION SIX

understanding of how we reach our final destiny. Perhaps this is new information. Perhaps Paul's teaching disturbs them because it challenges what they have been taught in the past. Invite participants to ponder their own journeys of faith as processes of transformation guided by the Holy Spirit.

Facilitator's Prayer

Gracious God, open my eyes and heart to see how you are guiding, shaping, and loving me into my ultimate destiny. Help me to let go of those things that stand in the way of your transformative power. Grant me the insight and eloquence to share my faith with the members of this group. Help me to be a good companion in their journeys of faith. In Jesus' name I pray. Amen.

Gather (10-15 minutes)

Check-in

Invite learners to share completed homework or any new thoughts or insights about the last session. Be ready to give a brief recap of that session if necessary.

Pray

Holy God, mighty and immortal, you are beyond our knowing, yet we see your glory in the face of Jesus Christ. Transform us into the likeness of your Son, who renewed our humanity so that we may share in his divinity, Jesus Christ our Lord, who lives and reigns with you and the Holy Spirit, one God, now and forever. Amen. (ELW, p. 26)

Focus Activity

Spend a few minutes contemplating the Focus Image. If the sun's reflection in the water was your only source of information about the sun, what would you know about the sun, and what information might you miss? If the sun's reflection on the paddle was your only source of information about the sun, what would you know about the sun, and what information might you miss? Is our perception of God more like looking at the sun, looking at reflections of the sun in the water, or looking at reflections of sun and water on the paddle?

Tip:
If group members prefer, they may add or substitute prayers of praise and/or petitions for renewal and transformation as needed in their lives.

Tip:
Invite participants to share their responses in small groups.

SESSION SIX

Open Scripture (10-15 minutes)

Gather a variety of items: letters written in ink, tablets of stone (or plaques), tablets of human hearts (candy hearts), veils, mirrors, light (flashlights or candles), symbols of Jesus (such as a cross), clay jars. (Be sure to have at least one item for each participant.) Invite each participant to select an item and hold it while listening to a volunteer read the text. How does the text speak about these items?

 OR

As volunteers read in turn 2 Corinthians 3:1-6; 3:7-11; 3:12-18; 4:1-6; 4:7-12; and 4:13-15; ask participants to jot down, doodle, or draw the image that touched them most deeply. Invite learners to share the significance of these images.

Read 2 Corinthians 3:1—4:15.

- What words, phrases, or images caught your attention?
- What questions does this passage raise?
- What is the tone of this passage? How does it make you feel?

Tip:
Instead of gathering items, you could display images on presentation slides while the text is read.

Join the Conversation (25-55 minutes)

Historical Context

1. People of Jewish faith observed the Law or Torah (Genesis, Exodus, Leviticus, Numbers, and Deuteronomy). While most early followers of Jesus were people of Jewish faith, this began to change as the gospel message spread to non-Jews (Gentiles). By the middle of the first century, the controversy that dominated the church, and Paul's ministry as well, involved admitting non-Jews into the church. This controversy reached the Corinthian congregation in the form of Jewish Christian apostles (2 Corinthians 11:22), who brought letters of recommendation (3:1) and visited the church in Paul's absence. These apostles insisted that Gentile believers abide by the Torah in order to be saved. This message was creating doubt and confusion among church members in Corinth.

- How would you imagine Gentile believers reacted to this message?

2. Paul heard about the activities of the Jewish Christian apostles and the confusion they were creating in the church. Today's text is part of his response.

Tip:
The 1998 "Guidelines" for Lutheran-Jewish Relations (available at www.elca.org/) state that although New Testament texts reflect early conflicts between Jesus' followers and other Jews, this must not be used to justify hostility towards present-day Jews or as a basis for depicting Judaism as legalistic.

Bonus Activity:
Read about the Jerusalem Council (49 C.E.) in Acts 15:1-35 and Galatians 2:1-14. Or view "Chapter 8: A Showdown in Christianity's Earliest History" from the *Frontline* documentary *From Jesus to Christ—The First Christians* (Pt. 1), at http://video.pbs.org/video/1365214164/.

SESSION SIX

Tip:
As a volunteer reads 2 Corinthians 3:1-16 slowly, use chart paper or a whiteboard to make two lists under the headings "New Covenant" and "Old Covenant."

Bonus Activity:
Many scholars believe that 2 Corinthians is not one letter, but a compilation of several letters or letter fragments. Take a quick look at the following Web sites to see how two different scholars deal with this issue:
- http://www.religiousstudies.uncc.edu/JDTABOR/cccorinthians.html
- http://www.paulonpaul.org/tent/ephesian_hq_2.htm

Tip:
Refer back to the chart in the Literary Context section of the Session Overview (p. 56).

- As 2 Corinthians 3:1-16 is read, list characteristics of the "new covenant" and "old covenant."
- Review the contrasts between the new and old covenants. What seems to be Paul's point? How is his message relevant in our own times?

Literary Context

1. Both sides of the debate over accepting Gentiles into the church appealed to the Hebrew Scriptures. In the session Scripture text, Paul draws upon Exodus 34 to make his case. In the story from Exodus, God tells Moses to bring two stone tablets to the top of Mount Sinai. There God gives the Ten Commandments and tells Moses to write the words on the stone tablets. When Moses comes down from the mountain with the commandments, his face reflects God's glory. Moses wears a veil over his face when he is among the people, but he removes the veil whenever he speaks with God.

- Read through 2 Corinthians 3:7—4:6. Fill in the rest of the chart below and discuss how Paul uses the text from Exodus to make his case. According to Paul, who or what is covered by a veil, and why? How is the veil removed?

Old covenant	New covenant
Stone tablets (2 Corinthians 3:3, 7; Exodus 34:1, 4)	Tablets of human hearts (2 Corinthians 3:3)
Old covenant of letters (2 Corinthians 3:14; Exodus 34:10-28)	(2 Corinthians 3:6)
Encountering God results in Moses' shining face (2 Corinthians 3:7; Exodus 34:29-30)	(2 Corinthians 3:8-11, 18)
The veil over Moses' face (2 Corinthians 3:13; Exodus 34:33)	(2 Corinthians 3:14-15)
Moses takes off the veil before the Lord (2 Corinthians 3:16; Exodus 34:34)	(2 Corinthians 3:14, 16)

2. Paul emphasizes that salvation is entirely the Holy Spirit's work by using images that contrast human fragility with the gospel's power. God enlightens and empowers us to overcome life's afflictions and in doing so joins us to the death and resurrected life of Jesus.

- Read 2 Corinthians 4:6-15. Underline images of human fragility and circle images of the gospel's power.

- In 2 Corinthians 4:11-12 Paul asserts that we carry in our bodies simultaneously the death and life of Jesus. How might this be part of the process of transforming us into the image of Christ (2 Corinthians 3:18)?

SESSION SIX

Lutheran Context

1. Martin Luther writes about the work of the Holy Spirit:

   I believe that by my own understanding or strength I cannot believe in Jesus Christ my Lord or come to him, but instead the Holy Spirit has called me through the gospel, enlightened me with his gifts, made me holy, and kept me in the true faith, just as he calls, gathers, enlightens, and makes holy the whole Christian church on earth and keeps it with Jesus Christ in the one common, true faith. (explanation of the Third Article of the Apostles' Creed, *Luther's Small Catechism with* Evangelical Lutheran Worship *Texts* [Augsburg Fortress, 2008], 16)

   - How do Luther's words help us understand Paul's message in the session Scripture text? Think of the different ways you hear people in church, in the media, and in society describe faith and the process of salvation. How is Paul's message relevant today?

2. Paul states that "the letter kills, but the Spirit gives life" (2 Corinthians 3:6). Martin Luther connects this to two kinds of preaching: law and gospel. He writes, "[I]t is impossible for someone who does not first hear the law and let himself be killed by the letter, to hear the gospel and let the grace of the Spirit bring him to life. . . . No one can have the one without the other" ("Concerning the Letter and the Spirit," in *Martin Luther's Basic Theological Writings*, 2nd ed., ed. Timothy F. Lull [Augsburg Fortress, 2005], 83). The law demands, accuses, and judges, in order to open us up to the promise, comfort, and grace of the gospel.

   - Review 2 Corinthians 3:1—4:15. Where do you hear law? Where do you hear gospel?

Devotional Context

1. Reflect back on the Focus Image. Jot down, doodle, or draw your responses to the following questions:

   - Where do you encounter the glory of the Lord? How?
   - How do you see God reflected in others?
   - How might others see God reflected in you?

2. Our ultimate destiny is to be like Christ and with Christ in God, who will be all in all. Today's session asks the question, "How do I achieve this glory?"

   - Name some ways that the session Scripture text affirms, surprises, or disturbs you and your understanding of salvation.

Bonus Activity:
Read about Exodus 34 in a commentary such as *Exodus (Interpretation: A Bible Commentary for Teaching and Preaching)* by Terence E. Fretheim (Westminster John Knox, 2010) or *The New American Commentary*, vol. 2, *Exodus*, by Douglas K. Stuart (Holman Reference, 2006). Compare this with Paul's treatment of Exodus 34.

Bonus Activity:
Compare 2 Corinthians 4:6 with Genesis 1:3; Psalm 112:4; and Isaiah 9:2. Is this a word-for-word quote or a paraphrase? How does Paul use these scriptural sources?

Bonus Activity:
Help participants gain more confidence in discerning law and gospel in the Bible by forming two teams, one to look at Exodus 20:1-17, and the other to look at Matthew 15:10-20. Who might hear the texts as law, and under what circumstances? Who might hear the texts as gospel, and under what circumstances?

Bonus Activity:
Discuss how Paul and Luther would respond to each of the following contemporary teachings:

- Decision theology: believers must make a decision for Christ, invite Christ into their hearts, dedicate their lives to Christ, and so on.
- Prosperity gospel: believers can obtain blessings of wealth and/or health by faithful payment of tithes and offerings or various acts.
- Works righteousness: believers earn God's grace by doing good works.

Tip:
Emphasize that law and gospel are more about the effects of God's Word on us than about the content of a particular Scripture passage. The same text can be both law and gospel to different people at the same time, or to the same person at different times.

SESSION SIX

Tip:
Have available paper and colored pencils or markers. As they feel comfortable, invite participants to share their jottings, doodles, or drawings for the first activity with the group.

Bonus Activity:
Sing or say together the words of the hymn "Change My Heart, O God" (ELW 801).

Tip:
Consider inviting participants to name out loud or silently in their hearts the specific things that are obstacles to their faith.

Tip:
Continue to encourage learners to journal about their thoughts and reflections on each session and the Homework and Enrichment activities.

- In your own words, summarize how 2 Corinthians 3:1—4:15 helps you understand how we become more like Christ. Who does all the work and who should get all the credit? How is the "old covenant" of the letter or the law helpful in this process?
- Give one example of how the Holy Spirit has been transforming you in your journey of faith.

Wrap-up

1. If there are any questions to explore further, write them on chart paper or a whiteboard. Ask for volunteers to do further research to share with the group at the next session.

2. As time allows, invite participants to reflect on what they have learned in this session. What new perspectives have they gained?

Pray

Come, Holy Spirit! Come into my life, be with me, and help me to see God more clearly in the world and in the people around me. Come, Holy Spirit! Come into my life, cleanse my heart, and help me to let go of those things—sins, opinions, habits, prejudices, possessions, or whatever they are—that keep me from loving you. Come, Holy Spirit! Come into my life, change me, mold me, and make me more and more like Jesus. Amen.

Extending the Conversation (5 minutes)

Homework

1. Read the next session's Bible text: 2 Corinthians 4:16—5:21.

2. Read Paul's description of the works of the flesh and the fruits of the Spirit in Galatians 5:16-26, and consider what the Holy Spirit is doing in your life. How can you open up more time and space in your life for the Holy Spirit's transformative work?

3. Organize a prayer group committed to helping each other develop the practice of daily prayer. Seek advice from your pastor or other spiritual leader or use a book like Martha Grace Reese's *Unbinding Your Heart: 40 Days of Prayer and Faith Sharing* (Chalice Press, 2008) to get started. Helpful resources are also available online:

- ELCA Prayer Center: www.elca.org/What-We-Believe/Prayer-Center.aspx
- Centering Prayer: www.centeringprayer.com

SESSION SIX

- Fixed-Hour Prayer: www.phyllistickle.com/fixedhourprayer.html
- "Centered by Prayer" article by Kimberly Winston: http://faithandleadership.duke.edu/features/articles/centered-prayer

Enrichment

1. If you want to read all of 1 and 2 Corinthians during this unit, read the following sections this week.
- Day 1: 2 Corinthians 3:1-18
- Day 2: 2 Corinthians 4:1-15
- Day 3: 2 Corinthians 4:16—5:10
- Day 4: 2 Corinthians 5:11-21
- Day 5: 2 Corinthians 6:1-13
- Day 6: 2 Corinthians 6:14—7:1
- Day 7: 2 Corinthians 7:2-16

2. Check out the following Web site for ideas about how to deepen your faith and spirituality: http://www.elca.org/Growing-in-Faith/Vocation/Rostered-Leadership/Leadership-Support/Health/Wholeness-Wheel.aspx. Read the quote from Martin Luther at the top of the page. Consider how this quote connects with 2 Corinthians 3:1—4:15. What does the Wholeness Wheel suggest about how the Holy Spirit is active in our lives?

3. Visit http://www.practicingourfaith.org/what-are-christian-practices and read about Christian practices that draw us into God's activity in the world and reflect God's grace and love.

For Further Reading

Dorothy C. Bass, *Practicing Our Faith: A Way of Life for a Searching People*, 2nd ed. (Jossey-Bass, 2010).

Robert Benson, *In Constant Prayer* (Thomas Nelson, 2008).

Lois Malcolm, *Holy Spirit: Creative Power in Our Lives* (Augsburg Fortress, 2009).

Looking Ahead

1. Read the next session's Bible text: 2 Corinthians 4:16—5:21.

2. Read through the Leader Guide for the next session and mark portions you wish to highlight for the group.

SESSION SIX

3. Make a checklist of any materials you'll need to do the Bonus Activities.

4. Pray for members of your group during the week.

SESSION SEVEN

2 Corinthians 4:16—5:21

Leader Session Guide

Focus Statement
In Christ we are invited to participate in God's mission of reconciliation.

Key Verse
So we are ambassadors for Christ, since God is making his appeal through us; we entreat you on behalf of Christ, be reconciled to God.
2 Corinthians 5:20

Focus Image

© thumb / iStockphoto

Reconciliation:
The end of estrangement between God and humanity, and/or between individuals and/or groups of persons; the reestablishment of friendly relations.

What Can I Do Here and Now?

Session Preparation

Before You Begin . . .

Take a few minutes to ponder the word *reconciliation*. What does it mean to you? Have you ever experienced it? What were the circumstances, and how did you feel? Are there situations or persons in your life that are not reconciled? If so, what would it take to make reconciliation a reality in those situations and with those persons? Do you have the ability to do it?

Session Instructions

1. Read this Session Guide completely and highlight or underline any portions you wish to emphasize with the group. Note any Bonus Activities you wish to do.

2. If you plan to do any special activities, check to see what materials you'll need, if any.

3. Have extra Bibles on hand in case a member of the group forgets to bring one.

Session Overview

Reconciliation is the main theme of this session. In 2 Corinthians 4:16—5:21 Paul describes the new covenant as being about God reconciling the world (all humanity and creation) to God's self. Learners will explore what reconciliation means and how God accomplishes it in Christ. They will be invited to see that being reconciled with God involves being called to take up a ministry of reconciliation in their own lives.

HISTORICAL CONTEXT

The session Scripture text is a continuation of Paul's teaching on the new covenant, which he insists is characterized by the activity of the Holy Spirit in the lives of believers, and not primarily by obedience to the laws of the Mosaic covenant.

As evidence of the Holy Spirit's presence in the lives of believers, Paul points to inner fortitude in the face of life's hardships. He insists that the Holy Spirit renews our spirits daily so that we are not crushed or driven to despair, forsaken or destroyed by the difficulties we encounter. In this way our lives begin to conform to the image of the crucified and resurrected Christ who walks

SESSION SEVEN

with us in the midst of adversity. Participants are encouraged to see similar patterns in their own lives.

Paul draws several contrasts here: between the outer nature that is wasting away and the inner nature that is being renewed daily, between momentary affliction and eternal glory, between visible and invisible, between temporary and eternal, between an earthly tent and a heavenly dwelling built by God, and between in the body/away from the Lord and away from the body/at home with God. However, Paul is not promoting Greco-Roman dualism in which our ultimate destiny is to shed our physical bodies like a set of dirty clothes. Instead Paul views our ultimate destiny more like moving out of a tent into a house or exchanging one set of clothing for another.

LITERARY CONTEXT

A word study is a way to approach a Scripture text from the literary perspective. It considers common definitions as well as unique ways that writers use particular words. In the session Scripture text, Paul uses two sets of terms—*renewed/new creation/reconciliation* and *judgment seat/recompense/fear of the Lord*—that can become clearer through a word study. The challenge for participants is to work out how these two sets of ideas, which may at first appear to be at cross-purposes, work together to achieve God's goal for humanity.

Ambassadors:
Official messengers or representatives who are called to be faithful to the one who sends them, remain disentangled from the customs of the place where they are sent, and return home at the appointed time.

This session's Literary Context also looks at the word **ambassadors**. Invite participants to explore what it means to be ambassadors, official messengers or representatives for Christ. In the world of politics and diplomacy, ambassadors are expected to be faithful to the country they represent, to not become entangled with customs where they are sent, and to return to their homeland at the appointed time. Are any of these ideas helpful to understanding our calling to be Christ's ambassadors? What should Christ's ambassadors be doing, if Christ's mission is reconciling the world to God?

The "happy exchange":
Christ has taken upon himself what belongs to me (my sin/brokenness) and given me what belongs to him (right relations with God and others).

LUTHERAN CONTEXT

Martin Luther's notion of the **"happy exchange"** between sinners and their Savior is the means by which God reconciles us to God's self. As we have seen throughout 1 and 2 Corinthians, this is not just a single event effected by baptism, but initiation into an ongoing lifelong transformative process. As reconciled sinners, we live no longer for ourselves but for Christ (2 Corinthians 5:15). What we do in our bodies—in other words, what we say and do every day—is the real-life tangible evidence that any kind of transformation is actually taking place.

"Cheap grace" is the idea that since God loves us just as we are and will forgive all our sins, nothing in our lives needs to change. What we do on Sunday morning has no implications for what we do during the rest of the week. Paul's insistence that God will indeed judge believers on the basis of what they have done in the body reminds us that although we are accepted by God just as we are (as sinners), God does not intend for us to remain sinners but wants to transform us into saints in the image of Christ.

Law and gospel refer to the effects of encountering God's Word. Law refers to our experience of Scripture as demands, expectations, and judgments. Gospel refers to our experience of the Word as comfort, grace, and healing. The Holy Spirit uses law to open us up to the transformative power of the gospel.

Devotional Context

In this context learners are invited to apply the session Scripture text to their own lives. Paul writes that "in Christ God was reconciling the world to himself, not counting their trespasses against them" (2 Corinthians 5:19). Here we see a model of what must happen if reconciliation is to take place. A key ingredient, in fact the only one Paul mentions, is God's amazing act of forgiveness—not counting our trespasses against us. Encourage your group to reflect on and discuss the need to forgive and let go of the past in order to create the possibility for a new and better future. How can we do this? What keeps us from doing this?

Facilitator's Prayer

Gracious God, thank you for all your gifts, especially for your Word made flesh, for your word in Scripture, and for your indwelling Holy Spirit. Help me to be an ambassador for Christ in this group today. Grant me the grace to forgive and to let go of the past in order to move on into the future that you are already preparing for us. Be with us as we gather in the name of your beloved Son, Jesus. Amen.

Gather (10-15 minutes)

Check-in

Invite learners to share completed homework or any new thoughts or insights about the last session. Be ready to give a brief recap of that session if necessary.

SESSION SEVEN

Tip:
Invite group members to offer prayers of praise for reconciliation achieved and/or petitions for reconciliation desired.

Tip:
Participants may be more comfortable journaling about these persons and situations in silence. When you invite them to share their thoughts, assure them that they do not have to reveal names or details about personal situations.

Pray

Grant, O God, that your holy and life-giving Spirit may move every human heart; that the barriers which divide us may crumble, suspicions disappear, and hatreds cease; and that, with our divisions healed, we might live in justice and peace; through your Son, Jesus Christ our Lord. Amen. (Evangelical Lutheran Worship, Pastoral Care [Augsburg Fortress, 2008], 381)

Focus Activity

Take a few moments to contemplate the message in the Focus Image. Journal your responses to the following questions:

- How does this message speak to you personally?
- Is this a message directed at you? If so, who is calling you to come back? Why?
- Is this a message you want to send to someone else? Why?

Open Scripture (10-15 minutes)

As a volunteer reads the Scripture passage slowly and with care, encourage learners to circle words or phrases that stand out to them.

Give each learner a lump of clay to mold or shape as desired while listening to the text as it is read.

Read 2 Corinthians 4:16—5:21.
- What words, phrases, or images touched you?
- How does this passage make you feel?
- What questions does this passage raise for you?

Join the Conversation (25-55 minutes)

Historical Context

1. In the session Scripture text, Paul continues to explain the nature of the new covenant, which consists of the experience and work of the Holy Spirit in the lives of believers, not obedience to the laws of Moses. The Spirit works to transform all (both Jewish and Gentile believers) into the image of Christ (2 Corinthians 3:18).

Tip:
A quick review of the Historical Context from Session 6 will help learners understand Paul's message in its original circumstances.

- Read 2 Corinthians 4:7—5:5 and note what the Holy Spirit guarantees and how the Spirit is active in the lives of believers. Is this how you experience the Holy Spirit in your life and in your journey of faith?

2. As mentioned in session 5, ancient Greeks and Romans believed that the soul escapes from the prison of the physical body when a person dies.
- Reread 2 Corinthians 4:16—5:9, paying close attention to Paul's language and metaphors. What point is Paul trying to make here about our ultimate destiny? Discuss how Paul's point of view compares or contrasts with ancient Greco-Roman beliefs.

Literary Context

1. Studying key words and phrases in a Scripture text can help us better understand the writer's message. In 2 Corinthians 4:16—5:21 Paul uses two sets of terms: *reconciliation, renewed,* and *new creation*; and *judgment, recompense,* and *fear of the Lord*. *Reconciliation* is commonly defined as the reestablishment of friendly relations; in theology it refers to ending the separation between God and humans caused by sin. *Renewed* and *new creation*, as Paul uses them here, suggest that God's goal is not to restore things to the way they were, but to create an entirely new set of relationships. *Judgment* involves evaluating evidence in light of particular values or desired outcomes. *Recompense* means reward or punishment ("getting our just desserts"). *Fear of the Lord* refers to a sense of wonder and awe in God's presence.
- Identify which words and phrases relate to the goal of God's mission in the world, and which ones point to how that goal will be accomplished. How do these two sets of words and ideas relate to one another? How do they come together in Paul's description of the new covenant?

2. Another key term in the session Scripture text is *ambassador*. In the world of politics and diplomacy, an ambassador is an official messenger or representative for a country. Ambassadors are expected to be faithful to the country they represent, to not become entangled with customs where they are sent, and to return to their homeland at the appointed time.
- Look up the word *ambassador* in a dictionary and reflect on what it means to be "ambassadors for Christ" (2 Corinthians 5:20). How does this fit with the ministry of reconciliation?

Bonus Activity:
Paul writes in more detail about the work of the Holy Spirit in the lives of believers in Galatians 5:13-26. Read this passage and invite participants to reflect on what the Holy Spirit is trying to accomplish in their lives.

Bonus Activity:
Paul uses the contrast between a tent and a building to distinguish between our current mortal bodies and the bodies we will receive in the resurrection. The author of Hebrews 11:8-12 uses the same terms. Compare and contrast the two passages.

Tip:
Have available some dictionaries or a computer that can be used to find definitions of the word *ambassador*.

Bonus Activity:
Ponder the scope of the reconciliation that God is accomplishing in Christ by reading Genesis 3. Take note of all the relationships in this chapter that are disrupted by sin. Consider how our ministry of reconciliation might include repairing our relationships not only with God and each other but with all of creation.

Bonus Activity:
Consider Jesus' instructions to the twelve apostles in Luke 9:1-6 and to the seventy in Luke 10:1-12. How do these instructions challenge our understanding of what it means to be an ambassador for Christ?

SESSION SEVEN

Tip:
Remind participants that each of us experiences law and gospel differently and according to where we are in our journey of faith.

Bonus Activity:
In light of the "happy exchange," take a few moments to contemplate Luther's commentary on Galatians 3:13 that Christ redeemed us by being "wrapped in our sins, our malediction, our death, and all our evils, as he is wrapped in our flesh and blood" (*A Commentary on St. Paul's Epistle to the Galatians* [Fleming H. Revell, 1961], 270).

Bonus Activity:
Take a few moments to look over the service for Corporate Confession and Forgiveness in ELW, pp. 238–242. Notice what happens right after the declaration of forgiveness. Discuss the practice of sharing the peace in light of the ministry of reconciliation that has been entrusted to us.

Tip:
Remind participants that sharing of personal situations is entirely voluntary.

Bonus Activity:
Discuss with your pastor how you might use the Corporate Confession and Forgiveness (ELW, pp. 238–242) in a closing activity.

Lutheran Context

1. Martin Luther's concept of the "happy exchange" explains how God reconciles us to God's self through Christ. It works like this: Christ has taken upon himself everything that belongs to us and has given to us everything that belongs to him. Consequently our sins are not reckoned to us but to Christ, and Christ gives his righteousness to us. In this life we remain sinners, but for Christ's sake God relates to us now as saints—at least saints in the making.

- If this is true, what is the purpose of God judging us according to the good and evil we have done while in the body (2 Corinthians 5:10)? What does judgment reveal about us and about God's grace?

2. Lutherans use the lenses of law and gospel to better understand Scripture. The law demands, accuses, and judges in order to open us up to the promise, comfort, and grace of the gospel. With your eyes closed, listen as someone reads aloud 2 Corinthians 4:16—5:21. What words of law and words of gospel do you hear? What does this suggest, if anything, about the condition of your relationship with God right now?

Devotional Context

1. Reconciliation is "a process of letting go of the past in order to live at peace in the future," according to William J. Danaher ("Some Reflections on the Theology of Reconciliation," http://www.elca.org/What-We-Believe/Social-Issues/Journal-of-Lutheran-Ethics/Issues/March-2004/Some-Reflections-on-the-Theology-of-Reconciliation.aspx).

- Discuss how this definition of reconciliation might help us better understand what God is doing by reconciling us and the world to God's self through Christ, what the ministry of reconciliation that has been entrusted to us is about, and what we need to do in order to be reconciled with God and with one another.

2. Take another look at the Focus Image and at what you wrote down during the Focus Activity. Discuss how the words "come back" are related to the ministry of reconciliation God is engaged in and which has been entrusted to us. What are some common obstacles to reconciliation?

Wrap-up

1. If there are any questions to explore further, write them on chart paper or a whiteboard. Ask for volunteers to do further research to share with the group at the next session.

2. Hand out a list of resources and/or contacts for marital, family, grief, and other forms of counseling that may be helpful to group members who are dealing with situations or persons in need of reconciliation.

Pray

Gracious God, help me trust in your steadfast love. Draw me back to you when I lose my way. Give me the courage to reach out to those I have hurt, and the grace to forgive those who have hurt me. Empower me to be an ambassador of Christ and a minister of reconciliation in my family, my workplace, my neighborhood, and my church, so that no one is left out of your embrace. In Jesus' name I pray. Amen.

Extending the Conversation (5 minutes)

Homework

1. Read the next session's Bible text: 2 Corinthians 8:1-15; 9:1-15.

2. Commit to seeking reconciliation with one person. Before contacting that person, spend some time reflecting on what happened in the past and what needs to be said or done (and by whom) in order to let go of the past so that you can have a relationship in the future. You may find it helpful to write all this down in a journal. Pray about it and ask for God's help. Then reach out to the person through a phone call, note, or e-mail inviting him or her to meet. Be clear about your reasons, hopes, and expectations for meeting. If the person agrees to a conversation, remember to listen as well as speak!

3. Consider organizing a small group to study and learn how to discuss difficult issues in your congregation. The following resources are available at http://www.elca.org/What-We-Believe/Social-Issues/Moral-Deliberation.aspx: "Talking Together as Christians about Tough Social Issues" and "Talking Together as Christians Cross Culturally: A Field Guide." Once your small group gains some confidence in doing this, ask each member to start and lead another small group.

Enrichment

1. If you want to read all of 1 and 2 Corinthians during this unit, read the following sections this week.
- Day 1: 2 Corinthians 8:1-15
- Day 2: 2 Corinthians 8:16—9:5

SESSION SEVEN

- Day 3: 2 Corinthians 9:6-15
- Day 4: 2 Corinthians 10:1-16
- Day 5: 2 Corinthians 10:17—11:15
- Day 6: 2 Corinthians 11:16—12:13
- Day 7: 2 Corinthians 12:14—13:10

2. Truth and reconciliation commissions have become a popular response to serious division and conflict in many countries. Search the Internet, beginning with Wikipedia, for articles on these commissions and the issues they have confronted. For an assessment of their success, view the documentary *Confronting the Truth: Truth Commissions and Societies in Transition* by Steve York and Neil J. Kritz (2007), available through the United States Institute for Peace Press (http://bookstore.usip.org).

3. Arrange for your group (along with others in your congregation) to view the movie *The Power of Forgiveness* (Journey Films, 2008). Discuss the role of forgiveness in processes of reconciliation. How does this connect with Paul's comments in 2 Corinthians 5:18-20?

For Further Reading

Kenneth Briggs, *The Power of Forgiveness* (Fortress Press, 2008).

Donald B. Kraybill, Steven M. Nolt, and David L. Weaver-Zercher, *Amish Grace: How Forgiveness Transcended Tragedy* (Jossey-Bass, 2010).

Looking Ahead

1. Read the next session's Bible text: 2 Corinthians 8:1-15; 9:1-15.

2. Read through the Leader Guide for the next session and mark portions you wish to highlight for the group.

3. Make a checklist of any materials you'll need to do the Bonus Activities.

4. Pray for members of your group during the week.

SESSION EIGHT

2 Corinthians 8:1-15; 9:1-15

Leader Session Guide

Focus Statement
God's grace produces blessings. Our response is gratitude in the form of thanksgiving to God and generosity toward those in need.

Key Verse
And God is able to provide you with every blessing in abundance, so that by always having enough of everything, you may share abundantly in every good work.
2 Corinthians 9:8

Focus Image

© Kirby Hamilton / iStockphoto

Grace:
In Lutheran theology grace refers to God's continuing action upon us. Grace comes to us once for all, again and again, more and more.

What Is My Response to God's Grace?

Session Preparation

Before You Begin . . .

Take a few moments to think about God's grace. What does God's grace mean to you? How have you experienced it today? What did it feel like in that moment? What effect has it had on your day overall? How have you responded to God's grace in your life today?

Session Instructions

1. Read this Session Guide completely and highlight or underline any portions you wish to emphasize with the group. Note any Bonus Activities you wish to do.

2. If you plan to do any special activities, check to see what materials you'll need, if any.

3. Have extra Bibles on hand in case a member of the group forgets to bring one.

Session Overview

Second Corinthians 8 and 9 are fragments of letters written by Paul reminding church members of their commitment to the relief of the saints in Jerusalem. Paul urges them to participate in this ministry in response to the **grace** they have experienced in their own lives. God's extravagant grace inspires us to share our gifts and resources with those who are in need. In this way we become agents of God's grace.

HISTORICAL CONTEXT

Paul's instructions in the session Scripture texts address his collection for the support of the church in Jerusalem. It is important for participants to understand that Jerusalem's economy revolved around the temple. Revenues from annual tithes, taxes, sales of sacrificial animals, currency exchange, and voluntary offerings supported the priests, Levites, security guards, and other temple staff. Many residents made a living by providing other services to the pilgrims who flocked to the city for religious festivals such as Passover. Largely shut out of this temple-based economy, the followers of Jesus appear to have lived off the proceeds of selling their property and possessions (Acts 2:43-47; 4:32-37). This would not have been a long-term sustainable

SESSION EIGHT

source of funds. Paul's comments in 2 Corinthians and elsewhere indicate that alleviation of economic hardship was the primary motive for the "ministry to the saints."

Participants will be asked to examine passages from 1 and 2 Corinthians and Paul's other letters. Here they will discover other possible motives for the collection, including a grateful response to the spiritual blessings the Gentiles have received (Romans 15:22-29) and/or a sign of the goodwill and unity between Gentiles and Jews in the church (Galatians 2:1-10). In addition, Paul's instructions and comments indicate that church members in Corinth and in the province of Macedonia were far from well off but could generate a surplus by setting aside small sums on a weekly basis.

LITERARY CONTEXT

In the session Scripture texts, which are fragments of letters written to the church at Corinth, we can discern Paul's motivational strategies. In 2 Corinthians 8:1-7 he summarizes the Macedonian success story, lifting up their generosity in the midst of extreme poverty. Paul draws on his knowledge of the Corinthian Christians—they are financially better off and have a competitive drive to excel—to motivate them to outdo the Macedonian churches in generosity. In 2 Corinthians 9:1-5 Paul reveals that he has been boasting about the Corinthian Christians' eagerness to participate in the collection. He wants them to know this because he is on his way to Corinth and is traveling with some Macedonian Christians. He does not want to be humiliated by the Corinthians not living up to his boasting.

Charis:
A Greek word used by Paul to describe both what God and Christ have done for us, and our human response. It is usually translated as "grace," "favor," "goodwill," "blessing," "generosity," or "thanksgiving."

Paul uses the Greek word ***charis*** to describe the goodwill and favor that God and Christ have toward humanity, and human responses to divine action. Hence the *charis* on behalf of the saints in Jerusalem (2 Corinthians 8:6) is a response to the *charis* of our Lord Jesus Christ (8:9). God provides us with every *charis* so that we may share abundantly in every good work (9:8). Our generosity in doing so produces *charis* to God (9:11). God's grace produces an eternal circle of grace given, received, and passed on.

LUTHERAN CONTEXT

Jesus' encounter with Zacchaeus in Luke 19:1-10 illustrates how grace comes to us, as Monica Jyotsna Melanchthon puts it, "once for all, again and again, and more and more." Consider the following:

- Zacchaeus is a rich tax collector, and therefore is one who has difficulty entering the kingdom (see Luke 18:24-25). Yet his

74   1, 2 Corinthians Leader Guide

SESSION EIGHT

name, Zacchaeus, means "the clean or righteous one." His public image is sinner, but his real name is saint.
- Zacchaeus wants to see Jesus. Why? (Think of Luther's explanation of the Third Article of the Apostles' Creed.)
- Jesus invites himself to stay in the house of Zacchaeus.
- Zacchaeus promises to give half of his wealth to the poor and to repay those he has defrauded four times what he took from them.

Participants will reflect on how this story helps us understand Paul's message and vice versa.

Philippians 2:6-11 and Romans 5:6-11 are expressions of Paul's theology of the cross, focusing on what Christ has done for us: humbling himself for our sakes, dying for us while we were still sinners to reconcile us to God. It is easy to associate these gifts of Christ with our ultimate destiny. In 2 Corinthians 8:9 Paul applies the same idea, expressed this time as Christ becoming poor so that we might become rich, to our daily lives. God's grace in Christ changes not only our ultimate destiny, but also how we live from day to day, how we use the gifts and blessings that come to us.

Devotional Context

The challenge for many people in our society is to see that all that we are and all that we have comes from God either directly or indirectly. We cannot choose the country, community, or family into which we are born. We may earn a living by using and developing our talents and skills, but we cannot choose what aptitudes come naturally or easily. Often we attribute our successes to luck, failing to see God's grace at work in the ordinary everyday things of life. Participants are invited to reflect on the blessings they have received and how they have used or are using those blessings.

An action-oriented group might enjoy the challenge of doing what Paul did—organizing a collection to meet the needs of people in the local, national, or global community. This activity could commit the group to working together beyond the timeframe of this Bible study as they make plans to involve others in this ministry.

Facilitator's Prayer

Gracious God, I am truly nothing without you. All that I am and all that I have ultimately come from you. Thank you for all that you have

SESSION EIGHT

given to me and to the members of this study group. As we continue to study your Word, may we encounter your grace again and again, more and more, so that we may be transformed to become agents of your grace. In Jesus' name I pray. Amen.

Gather (10-15 minutes)

Check-in

Invite learners to share completed homework or any new thoughts or insights about the previous session. Be ready to give a brief recap of that session if necessary.

Pray

Gracious God, you have given us so much. Teach us to appreciate your blessings and gifts. Help us to give generously and freely of all that you have given us. In Jesus' name we pray. Amen.

Focus Activity

Take a moment to reflect on the Focus Image. Name a wonderful gift you received from someone. How did you respond to this gift?

Tip: After the third sentence of the prayer, pause and invite group members to name things that have been bestowed on them as blessing and gift. After everyone has had an opportunity to do this, close with the last two lines of the prayer.

Open Scripture (10-15 minutes)

Place a collection plate or basket on a table in the center of the room to help learners visualize the point of these readings. (You have the option of using the collection plate/basket in the Devotional Context.)

Ask a volunteer to read 2 Corinthians 8:1-15. Pause to allow participants to reflect on the text before asking a second volunteer to read 2 Corinthians 9:1-15.

Read 2 Corinthians 8:1-15; 9:1-15.
- What words, phrases, or images caught your attention?
- What is the main topic or issue that Paul is addressing?
- What is your first response to this teaching?

SESSION EIGHT

Join the Conversation (25-55 minutes)

Historical Context

1. Aside from providing services to pilgrims visiting the temple for religious festivals, the city of Jerusalem had no significant industry or commercial base in biblical times. The temple derived revenue from tithes, offerings, and an annual tax collected by synagogues outside Judea. It is unlikely, however, that followers of Jesus in Jerusalem derived much, if any, economic benefit from the temple's activities. In the session Scripture texts, Paul encourages "the ministry to the saints"—a collection of funds for the support and relief of the church in Jerusalem.

- Read Paul's comments about this ministry in Galatians 2:1-10 and Romans 15:22-29. What other purposes might have been served by Paul's collection of funds for the Jerusalem church? What might the giving and receiving of this gift have symbolized?

2. Read 1 Corinthians 16:1-4 and 2 Corinthians 8:1-7. What do Paul's instructions suggest about the economic status of church members in the city of Corinth and in the Roman province of Macedonia? Are they much better off than church members in Jerusalem?

Literary Context

1. Many scholars regard 2 Corinthians as a compilation of fragments of letters that Paul wrote to the church over a period of a year or more. The session Scripture texts are two such fragments written at different times. They remind church members of their commitment to the collection for the saints in Jerusalem (1 Corinthians 16:1-4).

- Reread 2 Corinthians 8:1-9 and 9:1-7. How does Paul go about encouraging the members of the church to participate in the collection? What strategies does he use? Discuss whether you would find Paul's appeal persuasive.

2. Paul uses the Greek word *charis* and related terms repeatedly in the session texts. The New Revised Standard Version of the Bible translates this in various ways.

- Carefully reread the verses listed below. In each case, who is giving the *charis*, and who is receiving it? How are all these different uses of the word *grace* related to one another?

Tip:
The focus of this section is Paul's situation. Yes, the apostle was also a fundraiser! This may come as a surprise to some learners, but the reality is that the Bible talks about money a lot. One estimate is that there are as many as 2,350 verses in the Bible devoted to the topic of money.

Bonus Activity:
To read more about issues related to giving, visit the Web site http://www.biblegateway.com/resources/commentaries/IVP-NT/2Cor/Guidelines-Giving.

Bonus Activity:
Visit the following Web sites for more information on the economic situations in Corinth and Macedonia:
- http://gbgm-umc.org/umw/corinthians/city.stm
- http://www.unrv.com/provinces/macedonia.php

Tip:
You may decide to divide the learners into two small groups, assigning one activity to each group. Make sure to allow time for each group to report back to the whole.

Bonus Activity:
Explore the Web site http://www2.elca.org/stewardship/makeitsimple. Compare the strategy that is used here with that used by Paul to persuade believers to share their resources. How is the main message similar or different?

SESSION EIGHT

Bonus Activity:
Do you know where your weekly offering goes? See the pamphlet "Where Your Offering Goes" at www.elca.org/Growing-in-Faith/Discipleship/Stewardship.aspx and similar pamphlets available from your synod and/or congregational leaders.

Tip:
Use chart paper or a whiteboard to write down key words and points in your discussion.

Bonus Activity:
The notion of God's grace is deeply rooted in Scripture; it is referred to more than 200 times in the Old Testament alone. Read Psalm 103. How is God's grace demonstrated toward human beings, according to this ancient Israelite song? Reflect on how texts like this may have influenced Paul's understanding of what God was doing in Jesus Christ.

Bonus Activity:
As a group, write a prayer about grace received and grace extended to others.

> Summarize the point you think Paul is trying to make in repeating *charis* and related words.

Passage in 2 Corinthians	NRSV translation of *charis* and related terms
8:1; 9:14	"grace"
8:4	"privilege"
8:6-7, 19	"generous undertaking"
8:9	"generous act"
8:16; 9:15	"thanks"
9:8	"blessing"
9:11-12	"thanksgiving"

Lutheran Context

1. Martin Luther's emphasis on grace was the keystone of the Reformation, drawn from biblical texts such as Ephesians 2:8, "For by grace you have been saved through faith, and this is not your own doing; it is the gift of God." Luther insisted that grace is present at the beginning of faith, and is God's continuing action upon us. Grace comes to us "once for all, again and again, and more and more" (Monica Jyotsna Melanchthon, "The Grace of God and the Equality of Human Persons," *Dialog* [2003] 42, no. 1: 11).

- Read Luke 19:1-10. How do the actions of Zacchaeus relate to Luther's point about grace? How might Zacchaeus help us understand the point that Paul is making in 2 Corinthians 8:1-15 and 9:1-15?

2. Using the principle of "Scripture interprets Scripture," Lutherans look at other portions of Scripture to help interpret a particular text.

- Read Philippians 2:6-11 and Romans 5:6-11. How do these texts deepen your understanding of Paul's message in 2 Corinthians 8?
- Discuss Paul's claim that Christ's incarnation and cross are the basis of Christian generosity toward those in need. Restate this claim in a way that emphasizes grace.

Devotional Context

1. Spend a few moments reflecting on your life and experience in light of 2 Corinthians 9:8. Journal your responses to the following questions:

- What blessings have you received from God?
- What do you have that did not come from God either directly or through others?

- Why do you think God has blessed you with these things?
- What have you done with the blessings that God has bestowed upon you?
- What should you be doing with the blessings you have received?

2. Brainstorm a list of current local, national, or global needs. Commit to one need as a group. Take up a collection, beginning right now if possible. Make arrangements to involve others in this collection. Set a deadline for the completion of the collection. Spend some time preparing a flyer, a temple talk, or another communication media that you can share with others.

Tip:
If a collection of money is not doable in your setting, consider collecting toys, books, coats, blankets, or other needed items.

Bonus Activity:
Visit www.globalrichlist.com, enter a dollar figure such as $50,000 (roughly the average annual income in the U.S.), and discover how rich that is on a comparative global scale.

Wrap-up

1. If there are any questions to explore further, write them on chart paper or a white board. Ask for volunteers to do further research to share with the group at the next session.

2. If your group has decided to take up a collection, encourage participants to set up an accountability structure to ensure that the project is completed in a timely fashion.

Pray

God of abundance, you have poured out a large measure of earthly blessings: our table is richly furnished, our cup overflows, and we live in safety and security. Teach us to set our hearts on you and not these material blessings. Keep us from becoming captivated by prosperity, and grant us wisdom to use your blessings to your glory and to the service of humankind; through Jesus Christ our Lord. Amen. (ELW, p. 80)

Extending the Conversation (5 minutes)

Homework

1. Each day during the coming week, meditate on 2 Corinthians 9:8. In your journal, write down how God has blessed you that day.

2. Commit yourself to the practice of gratitude and thanksgiving. Take some time each day to contact one person who has been a blessing to you.

3. Luther's explanation of the eighth commandment calls us to practice generosity of speech. Commit yourself to this spiritual

discipline for the next week, and ask God to give you a generous spirit.

Enrichment

1. Watch the movie *Pay It Forward* (Warner Brothers, 2000), reflecting how good works done without expectation of a payback (in other words, grace) can change people's lives for the better.

2. Get involved in your congregation's stewardship ministry. Visit the Web site http://www2.elca.org/stewardship/makeitsimple for ideas about stewardship education and events for all ages.

3. If you are more of a history buff, enjoy a recap of Paul's ministry by viewing *Peter and Paul and the Christian Revolution*, available at www.pbs.org/peterandpaul.

For Further Reading

Bradley Hanson, *A Graceful Life: Lutheran Spirituality for Today* (Augsburg Fortress, 2000).

Mark Allan Powell, *Giving to God: The Bible's Good News about Living a Generous Life* (Eerdmans, 2006).

www.ingramcontent.com/pod-product-compliance
Lightning Source LLC
Chambersburg PA
CBHW051421070526
44584CB00023B/3530